POVERTY: THE

Carey Oppenheim

1965-1990

CHILD POVERTY ACTION GROUP **25** YEARS *Working against poverty*

CPAG 1-5 BATH STREET, LONDON EC1V 9PY

CPAG promotes action for the relief, directly or indirectly, of poverty
among children and families with children. We work to ensure that
those on low incomes get their full entitlements to welfare benefits.
In our campaigning and information work we seek to improve
benefits and policies for low income families, in order to eradicate
the injustice of poverty. If you are not already supporting us, please
consider a donation, or ask for details of our membership schemes
and publications.

Child Poverty Action Group
1-5 Bath Street, London EC1V 9PY

ISBN 0 946744 28 9

Cover and design: Devious Designs, Stafford Road, Sheffield
Typesetting: Boldface Typesetters, 17A Clerkenwell Road, London EC1
Printing: Calvert's Press, Redchurch Street, London E2

Contents

Preface

The Child Poverty Action Group is 25 years old this year. CPAG was set up in 1965 by a small group of people who were concerned about poverty amongst families with children in the affluent UK in the sixties. Since then, CPAG has grown to become an organisation of over 5,000 members, over 20 staff, and over 50 branches throughout the country. But our main aims have remained the same: to make poverty a central issue for politicians and the public; to highlight how poverty affects children in particular; to help low-income families get the most out of the current system of welfare benefits; to monitor the impact of legislation on those in poverty, especially families; and to argue for policies to bring about a fairer future for all our children.

As we enter the 1990s, we are faced in some ways with a situation similar to that faced by CPAG when it was founded 25 years ago. The UK's prosperity is growing. New developments in technology potentially mean a leap forward in productivity and communications. Many people are becoming much better off. And yet there is a substantial minority in the UK who live on low incomes and are likely to be excluded both from an acceptable standard of living today and from a fair share of the progress and prosperity of the future.

Poverty: the Facts aims to give a picture of poverty in the UK today, concentrating in particular on children and families. Whilst it has been a regular publication over the last few years, this is an expanded version, produced specially for CPAG's 25th anniversary. We have tried not only to give a perspective on the extent of poverty but also to convey what living in poverty actually means for those who experience it – the texture of poverty as well as the facts and figures. CPAG believes that greater public awareness is essential to the creation of a commitment to a comprehensive attack on poverty in the 1990s. Our objective in producing *Poverty: the Facts* is to increase that awareness, as a first step to significant change towards freedom from poverty and the fear of poverty for all.

The first question CPAG is usually asked by the media and other en-
quirers is 'what is poverty?' The second is ' how many people live in
poverty in this country today?' The answer to the first question CPAG
has always known: people live in poverty when they are excluded form
participating in the accepted way of life in the society in which they live.
The answer to the second question – what is the exact 'poverty line'
which divides the poor from the rest? – is always more problematic,
especially in a country such as ours in which no government has ever
recognised an official poverty line.

The precise definition of a 'poverty line' is bedevilled by lack of adequate information from official sources; by technical arguments, which
sometimes seem to amount to calculating how many angels can dance on
the head of a pin; and ultimately by the unresolvable nature of the question itself. It is probably as much of a delusion to believe that there will
ever be complete agreement on a definition of a 'poverty line' as to
believe that there will be complete agreement on the best way to solve
poverty.

What we do in *Poverty: the Facts* is to look at two of the possible
definitions of a 'poverty line'. First, we look at 50% of average income,
the lowest level of income analysed in the Government's *Households
below Average Income* figures, and the same as the 'poverty line' used
for comparisons across the European Community. Secondly, we look at
figure for the same year (1987) published by the Institute for Fiscal
Studies; these examine the numbers on and below the supplementary
benefit level of income and we look at the supplementary benefit level as
another 'working' definition of a 'poverty line'.

We also discuss other methods for arriving at a 'poverty line' which
provide a useful way forward: the examination, on as objective a basis as
possible, of what level of income is needed to participate in today's complex and wealthy society; and research into what the population in
general sees as necessities without which people are seen as living below
an acceptable minimum. Such studies as have been done in the past on
either basis have tended to produce definitions of a poverty level income
higher than either of the two definitions described above.

What *Poverty: the Facts* shows is that, on any of these definitions, the
numbers of people in poverty in the UK in recent years run into millions;
and that the levels of income which they have to survive on means that
they are denied the possibility of access to goods and resources which any
affluent and civilised society ought to be able to provide them with.

CPAG believes that this situation should be regarded as intolerable. In
particular, we believe that the blighting of so many children's lives, and

the blunting of their expectations, which result from poverty should not be tolerated by any of us. An understanding that poverty is rooted in the way our society is organised, rather than in individuals' personal characteristics – that it is about injustice, rather than inadequacy – is needed as a basis for a concern about poverty to be converted into a commitment to change. There is some evidence that in this country that understanding is now developing. From very punitive attitudes towards poor people in the mid 1970s, it seems from a recent EEC-wide study that people in the UK are now more likely to blame society's structures and less likely to blame those in poverty themselves.

But the final ingredient in a recipe for real change is a belief that it is possible to take effective action against poverty – that something can be done. This where CPAG comes in again. We spread information about the extent of poverty and combat the attitudes which blame poor people themselves for their poverty. But we also try to show, by our own everyday activities, that change is possible. Small victories – winning benefit rights, persuading a local council to alter its policies affecting poor families – lay the foundations for a broader change in priorities.

In the run-up to the next election, CPAG aims to ensure that all the main political parties put strategies to achieve freedom from poverty for all at the top of their agendas. We will be arguing for the defence and extension of rights, to create greater fairness and social justice in this country. We believe that all our children deserve the chance of real change towards a fairer future. We hope that all the readers of this book will support CPAG in our work to that end.

Fran Bennett
Director, Child Poverty Action Group

Acknowledgements

Many thanks to the many people who contributed to this book. Thanks to Fran Bennett, Peter Golding, Julia Lewis, David Piachaud, Peter Townsend and Peter Wiles for their very valuable comments on the manuscript. In particular thanks to David Piachaud who patiently helped with my many quries and to Fran who kept my ordinary work at bay and vigilantly proofed large chunks of text.

We consulted many people on the difficulties of choosing a poverty line. Many thanks to Tony Atkinson, Jonathan Bradshaw, John Hills, Ruth Lister, David Piachaud, Garry Runciman, Peter Townsend, John Veit Wilson and CPAG's Executive Committee for their wisdom and advice. The responsibility for the final text lies, of course, with us.

Special thanks to Richard Kennedy and Julia Lewis who spend enormous amounts of time and energy suggesting ideas for the book and editing it. Many thanks to Peter Ridpath for the promotion of the book, to Pat Shillong for the thankless task of typing in changes to the manuscript, to Nigel Taylor for the beautiful work he has done on the design and graphs, to Boldface Typesetters and Calverts for producing the book at breakneck speed. And finally thank you to Bill Norris and everyone to CPAG for their patience and all their support.

Introduction

Beneath the veneer of our affluent society the scars of poverty are at times obvious, at other times hidden.

Restaurant owners on the Strand in London plan to employ a cleaning firm to flood out, like so much rubbish, homeless young people who have had to make the pavements their home. The restaurant-goer will no longer have to step over the sleeping bodies of the young homeless. In the railway and tube stations, beggars of all ages and backgrounds have become the norm rather than the exception. These shocking images are the more visible signs of the poverty and inequality of our capital city.

But poverty is not always so dramatic, so visible to the passer-by. Poverty is also hidden away inside homes, institutions and workplaces. It is not just a feature of the North or inner cities, but widespread throughout the affluent regions and rural areas. In 1987 over 10 million people, nearly a fifth of the population in Britain, were living in poverty – measured by *either* of the most common definitions. In 1979 4.9 million people, nearly a tenth of the population in Britain, were living in poverty (defined as incomes below 50% of average). [1]

In the last decade, the gulf separating poverty from affluence has increased dramatically, reinforced by generous tax cuts on the one hand and decidedly ungenerous social security policies on the other. Between 1979 and 1987, the richest fifth of society saw their share of total household income (after taxes and cash benefits) *rise* from 40% to 45%; the poorest saw theirs *fall* from 6.1% to 5.1%. [2] For the first time since the Second World War the poorest half of the population have found that their share of total income is dropping. [3]

Why has there been such an increase in poverty and inequality?

Firstly, between 1979 and 1986, unemployment tripled to over 3 million people. The exodus of manufacturing industry from some parts of the country – such as the North, the North-West and the Midlands – has meant whole towns devastated by the closure of a steel foundry, a textile factory, or a coal mine. Many inner cities have been emptied of their old industries and crafts. Large-scale redundancies brought poverty in their wake: associated industries closed down and small shopkeepers shut up shop when people cut their spending. Although the catastrophic levels of unemployment in the mid-eighties have temporarily subsided, unemployment is on the rise once again.

Secondly, the nature of employment itself has changed radically. The recent industrial transformation which brought such stubbornly high levels of unemployment has reshaped the labour market. Part-time work and self-employment have grown substantially. Temporary and casual work has also increased. This type of work is frequently low paid with poor working conditions and few employment and social security rights. This has particularly serious implications for women who make up the majority of part-time employees. Policies which have abolished employment rights and protection for wages have facilitated the proliferation of low pay. It is harder to capture the reality of poverty in work – long hours, cramped working conditions, juggling two jobs, coping with working and looking after children and meagre rates of pay. For many, poverty is about grappling with the insecurities and frustrations associated with spells of unemployment interspersed with low-paid work. Such work patterns taint the present with poverty and offer no respite for the future.

Thirdly, these profound economic changes have gone hand in hand with shifts in family patterns.[4] In 1987, 14% of all families with children were single parents – a rise from 12% in 1979 and 8% in 1971. Nine out of ten single parents are women. Trapped by the frequent combination of low wages and the difficulty of finding childcare, many single mothers face a bleak future reliant on inadequate benefits.

Fourthly, the social security system has become an increasingly inadequate tool to deal with today's problems. Designed for a full-time male workforce, it discriminates against those who have been low paid, or unemployed, against those who have worked part time and people who have come to this country from abroad. The most radical reform of social security since Beveridge was fully implemented in 1988. It swallowed up rights and reduced benefits for some of the poorest in the country, weakening social security protection still further.

While we are daily besieged by evidence of the hardship and harsh conditions that people endure, some policy makers and commentators argue that poverty is 'a thing of the past', a product of the fevered imagination of the 'poverty lobby'. For others, poverty is symbolised by the growth of a so-called 'underclass' or the 'undeserving poor' who have brought their poverty upon themselves. But as the pages which follow demonstrate – the facts about poverty speak for themselves; and the causes of poverty are primarily structural rather than personal.

> My name is Bijon. I am coming up to nine years of age . . . poverty means not having what you need. You have outer needs and inner needs, such as your body needs a house and food and toys and your soul needs friendship and happiness and prayer and mediation. We are poor in money compared to most people in our town. But we are rich compared to homeless people and starving people . . . For us being poor means you have less and less. When things break you can't mend them or get new ones. First the lawnmower broke so the grass is all long. I call it the field. Then the van failed the MOT. I miss the van most. No more adventures or weekends at Gran's unless she sends the fare. [5]

Poverty means going short materially, socially and emotionally. It means spending less on food, on heating, and on clothing than someone on an average income. But it is not what is spent that matters, but what isn't. Poverty means staying at home, often being bored, not seeing friends, not going to the cinema, not going out for a drink and not being able to take the children out for a trip or a treat or a holiday. It means coping with the stresses of managing on very little money, often for months or even years. It means having to withstand the onslaught of society's pressure to consume. It impinges on relationships with others and with yourself. Above all, poverty takes away the tools to build the blocks for the future – your 'life chances'. It steals away the opportunity to have a life unmarked by sickness, a decent education, a secure home and a long retirement. It stops people being able to plan ahead. It stops people being able to take control of their lives.

So poverty widens the gap between reality and potential. But despite poverty, people struggle to make do with strength, resilience and dignity in the face of immense difficulties.

In *Poverty: the Facts* we can only touch on some of these issues, yet the themes we explore lie at the heart of CPAG's work. CPAG fights for a society free from poverty. Part of our role is act as both witness and reporter, to explain the causes of poverty, and to portray poverty to a wider audience. Armed with the facts we can argue for a society which puts an end to the exclusion of millions from society; we can argue for a society which recognises the right of all to an adequate income from employment or benefit allowing people to participate in society as full members.

This book is intended to guide the reader to the most important facts and figures about poverty today. It looks at official and independent data on poverty and low incomes, the causes and reality of poverty, poverty for women and for black and minority groups, inequalities, disparities between the countries and regions of the United Kingdom and how we compare to the rest of Europe. In doing so, it draws on the work of researchers, academics, and government statisticians, as well as the views of ordinary people.

NOTES

1. DSS, *Households below Average Income: a statistical analysis 1981-1987*, Government Statistical Service, 1990.
2. *Economic Trends*, May 1990, HMSO, 1990.
3. A B Atkinson, *The Department of Social Security's Report on Households below Average Income 1981-1987*, Paper for the Social Services Select Committee, 1990.
4. K Kiernan and M Wicks, *Family Change and Future Policy*, Family Policy Studies Centre and Joseph Rowntree Memorial Trust, 1990.
5. Bijon Chaudhuri, winner of CPAG/Young Guardian competition in April 1989, printed in *Poverty*, No 73, CPAG Ltd, summer 1989.

ONE

Definitions and debates

Definitions: what is poverty?

> *Poverty is not only about shortage of money. It is about rights and relationships; about how people are treated and how they regard themselves; about powerlessness, exclusion and loss of dignity. Yet the lack of an adequate income is at its heart.*
>
> Faith in the City [1]

Homeless people sleeping under the arches, pensioners counting out the pennies in the supermarket. A family crowded into a single room in a bed and breakfast hotel, mothers stretching out child benefit until their next giro comes. The fear of the debt collector, the queues for a housing transfer, for benefit, for advice . . . there is no doubt that these are the manifestations of poverty. However, in other respects poverty is difficult to define. For example, how does poverty in Britain compare to poverty in Ethiopia? How is the perception of poverty modified from one generation to the next? Is poverty for one family the same as poverty for another? Is poverty experienced in the same way by men and women?

British governments of all political persuasions have refused to define an official 'poverty line'. As a consequence, there is no *official* yardstick for measuring the rise or fall in poverty under different governments. This said, we can identify three broad approaches to defining poverty.

Absolute poverty

An *absolute* definition of poverty assumes that it is possible to define a minimum standard of living based on a person's *biological* needs for food, water, clothing and shelter. The emphasis is on basic physical needs and not on broader social and cultural needs. Absolute poverty is when people fall below this level, when they cannot house, clothe or feed themselves.

Seebohm Rowntree used an absolute definition of poverty in his study of poverty in York in 1899. He devised a 'primary' poverty line based on a standard of minimum needs for food, clothing, heating and rent, to show that many families had incomes below this level. But, as he himself wrote:[2]

> My primary poverty line represented the minimum sum on which physical efficiency could be maintained. It was a bare standard of *subsistence* rather than living . . . such a minimum does not by any means constitute a reasonable living wage.

In spite of its obvious limitations, the absolute view of poverty is still a definition valued by many commentators. For example, Lord Joseph (former Secretary of State for Social Services) argued:[3]

> An absolute standard of means is defined by reference to the actual needs of the poor and not by reference to the expenditure of those who are not poor. A family is poor if it cannot afford to eat . . . A person who enjoys a standard of living equal to that of a medieval baron cannot be described as poor for the sole reason that he has chanced to be born into a society where the great majority can live like medieval kings. By any absolute standards there is very little poverty in Britain today.

The appeal of an absolute definition of poverty is its apparent clarity. If there is not enough to eat there is poverty. However, it is very difficult to define an 'adequate' minimum when standards of living themselves change over time. How we house, clothe and feed ourselves has changed drastically over the years. Living standards also vary radically in different cultures. People's expectations also change, so that a minimum standard of living is shaped by the way society as a whole behaves and spends its money. Thus, 'an adequate minimum' is itself defined by what is socially acceptable. Such considerations demand a more sophisticated approach to the definition of poverty.

Relative poverty

> Poor people in Britain are not, of course, as poor as those in the Third World. But their poverty is real enough nonetheless. For poverty is a relative, as well as an absolute concept. It exists, even in a relatively rich Western society, if people are denied access to what is generally regarded as a reasonable standard and quality of life in that society.   (*Faith in the City*)[4]

In this instance poverty is defined in relation to a generally accepted standard of living in a specific society at a specific time and goes beyond basic biological needs. This view of poverty has a long heritage. Adam Smith, the eighteenth century economic philosopher, commented:[5]

> By necessities I understand not only commodities which are indispensably necessary for the support of life but whatever *the custom of the country* renders it indecent for creditable people, even of the lowest order, to be without.   (our emphasis)

In 1979, Peter Townsend's definitive work, *Poverty in the UK*[6], provided a forceful presentation of a relative view of poverty which echoed Smith's concerns:

> Individuals . . . can be said to be in poverty when they lack the resources to obtain the types of diet, participate in the activities and have the living conditions and amenities which are customary, or at least widely encouraged or approved, in the societies to which they belong.

Thus poverty is not simply about lack of money but also about exclusion from the customs of society. While there are a number of difficulties inherent in this approach – for example, how do we establish what the norms of our society are, or what people *choose* to manage without? – such a perspective has played a crucial role in establishing a new agenda for contemporary debates about poverty.[7]

The relative view of poverty has been shared by people across the political spectrum. For example, when she was Conservative social security minister, Lynda Chalker MP said:[8]

> It is not sufficient to assess poverty by absolute standards; nowadays it must be judged on relative criteria by comparison with the standard of living of other groups in the community . . . beneficiaries must have an income which enables them to participate in the life of the community.

Relative poverty is about social exclusion imposed by an inadequate income. It is not only about having to go short of food or clothing, it is also about not being able to join a local sports club, or send your children on a school trip, or go out with friends , or have a Christmas dinner:

> Christmas is not a time for celebrating for our family as we can only manage to buy the bare basic things to tide us over the holiday period. We do manage to buy a chicken for Christmas Day, that's all. After that it's back to basic meals – egg and chips, sausage and mash etc. We cannot even afford trivial things like jellies, mince pies, crackers etc to brighten up the festive season.
>
> (Mother of two, London)[9]

A consensual view of poverty

In *Poor Britain*, Joanna Mack and Stewart Lansley adopted a new approach to poverty in which social consensus was used as a guide. [10] In a development of the relative approach, they defined being in poverty as a situation in which people had to live without the things which society as a whole regarded as necessities. They found that there was general agreement about what constituted a minimum standard of living. At least two out of three people thought the following were necessities:

- Self-contained damp-free accommodation with an indoor toilet and bath
- A weekly roast joint for the family and three daily meals for each child
- Two pairs of all-weather shoes and a warm, waterproof coat
- Sufficient money for public transport
- Adequate bedrooms and beds
- Heating and carpeting
- A refrigerator and washing machine
- Enough money for special occasions like Christmas
- Toys for the children

In 1983, they found that 7.5 million people – 1 in 7 of the population – lacked three of these necessities or more.

The limitations of the traditional debates about poverty have obscured crucial aspects of poverty, in particular poverty *inside* families. Recent research has found that women are much more vulnerable to poverty than men, but that their poverty has been hidden by surveys which have ignored individual living standards within the home (see Chapter 6).

CPAG has always supported the view that poverty should also be seen in relation to the standard of living in a particular society. People should have a right to an income which allows them to *participate* in society rather than merely exist. Such participation involves having the means to fulfil responsibilities to others such as partners, sons and daughters, to care for elderly or sick relatives, to help neighbours and friends, and be able to join in as workers and citizens:

> People should be given enough money so that they can actually live a life that's reasonably comfortable – so they can do things they enjoy and not just survive, because everybody has a right to more than survive.
>
> (Unemployed worker) [11]

Debates: the poverty controversy

Ever more pronounced social division has brought poverty to the headlines and provoked widespread discussion. We discuss four themes which have run through recent debates: the view that poverty has been solved through economic progress, the disappearance of the word 'poverty', poverty as 'dependency' and the rise of the 'underclass'.

The end of the line for poverty

The debate about poverty exploded in the spring of 1989. John Moore MP, the then Secretary of State for Social Security, claimed that economic success had put an end to *absolute* poverty – in the sense of hunger, lack of shelter, overcrowding – and that *relative* poverty, a concept he claimed was invented by academics in the sixties, simply meant inequality. Moore argued: [12]

> . . . by almost every material measure it is possible to contrive: health, longevity, real income, ownership of consumer durables, number and length of holidays, money spent on entertainment, numbers in further education . . . not only are those with lower incomes not getting poorer, they are substantially better off than they have ever been before . . . It is capitalism that has wiped out the stark want of Dickensian Britain . . . It is capitalism that has caused the steady improvements in the living standards throughout this century . . . It is capitalism which is the only firm guarantee of still better living standards for our children and our grandchildren . . .

The speech was greeted by a storm of protest. 'Poor Better off without Moore', 'Moore's New Poor Lore', 'Threadbare or Feckless?', ran the headlines of the day. The speech touched a raw nerve – the government's assertions coincided with growing visible evidence of public squalor and individual poverty. Whatever facts and figures were produced to justify the claims of the 'end of poverty', there was no doubt in the minds of both the people living in poverty and those who witnessed it at close quarters that nothing could be further from the truth. To those people, poverty was desperately real and increasingly conspicuous.

In addition, far from being the invention of sixties' academics out to discredit capitalism, relative poverty, as we have seen, was a well established concept promoted in the eighteenth century by free-market enthusiast Adam Smith.

The starting point for this type of approach to poverty is the conviction that economic growth is the answer to poverty. The 'trickle-down' theory, as it is popularly known, is the belief that economic prosperity will filter down to the poorest and that a rising tide will lift all boats. As one of the theory's more passionate advocates has said: 'The market will provide a constantly rising set of minimum standards including rising minimum standards of income.' [13]

But there are a number of problems with this approach. Firstly, while it is true that 'Dickensian poverty' is largely a thing of the past, absolute poverty does still exist. There are still people without shelter; families are still crammed into single rooms; and people still go short of food. Secondly, there is no evidence that a booming economy automatically benefits the poorest in society. In fact, recent figures from the Department of Social Security show that, between 1979 and 1987 the real incomes of the poorest 10% went up by just 0.1% (after housing costs) in comparison with a rise of 23% for the average. Even before housing costs the real incomes of the average went up by nearly three times that of the poorest 10%. [14] Thirdly, there is a different approach which argues that the poorest are entitled to a fair share of the growth in prosperity.

And finally, relative poverty is not the same as inequality. Relative poverty is concerned with minimum needs which are established by the prevailing standards in our society; it is not about the gap between rich and poor. It is logical (though perhaps not desirable) to argue that the poorest fifth of the population should have higher incomes in order to be able to participate more fully in society, while accepting vast affluence at the other end of the income scale. Thus, there is no automatic link between the relative definition of poverty and the pursuit of greater equality.

Poverty? What poverty?

One of the more disturbing characteristics of recent years has been the disappearance of the word 'poverty'. Government documents no longer use the term but have replaced it with bland euphemisms – 'low income', 'below average income', 'the bottom ten per cent' – which smother the reality of deprivation, poverty and hardship. This has happened alongside changes in the so-called 'poverty statistics' (see Chapter 2) which have made it more difficult to find a consensus on what constitutes poverty. But perhaps the most explicit attempt to do away with the concept of poverty came with the Prime Minister's statement in a letter to the Leader of the Opposition: [15]

> I have too much respect for ordinary people to belittle those who receive income support or to denigrate children in families receiving income support by

the use of labels like 'poverty'. I firmly believe that the best way to help everyone is through encouraging them to take pride in themselves and to make use of their talents rather than alienating them, making them feel helpless and encouraging dependency on the state.

It is true that some people living in poverty do not call themselves 'poor'. Even if they have very little money, they may see themselves instead as pensioners, or single parents or tenants. But if the word 'poverty' is obliterated from public discussion, the experience of people in poverty disappears from our perception of social reality. It then becomes politically possible to stand up and say that in effect there is no poverty.

Dependency

We believe that dependence in the long run decreases human happiness and reduces human freedom. We believe the well-being of individuals is best protected and promoted when they are helped to be independent, to use their talents to take care of themselves and their families, and to achieve things on their own, which is one of the greatest satisfactions life can offer . . . Everyone knows the sullen apathy of dependence and can compare it with the sheer delight of personal achievement.   (Rt Hon John Moore MP)[16]

While the word 'poverty' has disappeared from the government's vocabulary, it has developed a new language to describe the condition of being poor – that of 'dependency'. It seems that 'dependency' is not due to unemployment, or low wages, or bringing up a child as a single parent, but is the result of long-term reliance on state help. In other words, welfare itself generates poverty. The introduction of the social fund in 1988 was promoted in language which stressed an end to 'dependency'. The fund primarily provides loans instead of grants for income support claimants to purchase large items , which could not be bought out of their basic benefit. The government's view was that:[17]

We believe that it is right in principle to (introduce) the concept of loans . . . because it has been a consistent objective of the (benefit) reforms to give people a sum of money within which they manage for themselves, *reducing their dependence on the 'benefit culture' for extras.*

(Rt Hon Nicholas Scott MP – our emphasis)

There are several objections to this approach. Firstly, many claimants do not *want* to rely on state benefits but have little choice because of few employment or training opportunities, the poverty trap, inadequate childcare facilities and so on. Secondly, the government's stigmatisation of dependency is extremely limited, since it focuses solely on the reliance on benefits. Reliance on tax subsidies (for example, mortgage interest tax relief) is not seen as dependency. The Conservative Bow Group put the point very clearly: [18]

> [the] debate . . . on the dependency problem . . . has started in a worryingly if not wholly surprisingly blinkered way. The images conjured up . . . are those of the unmarried teenage mother in a council flat, the long-term unemployed industrial worker and his family: whereas a full account should include pictures of the middle-class family drawing no welfare benefits or dole, but mortgaged up to the eye balls.

Thirdly, policies which aim to reduce dependence on certain kinds of state support often push people into greater dependence on families, friends, relatives and charity or leave them without support at all. For example:

> I applied to the social fund for £60 for carpets, but they refused . . . I asked me dad and he said 'No'. My nan and grandad also said 'No'.
> (Hilary, single mother) [19]

> If we have a crisis I've got no one to turn to, as my family and friends live so far away.
> (Mary, single mother) [20]

Thus, dependency does not vanish with the erosion of support from the state, but simply finds a new focus. Finally, it is absurd to consider independence and dependence as anything other than relative terms. We are all mutually dependent – some of us for life because of a severe disability, others at particular times and in specific circumstances:

> It could be argued that dependency and vulnerability are endemic features of the human condition and the question then is how these dependencies are to be handled, whether through the state or more through private charity and voluntary sector provision.
> (Raymond Plant) [21]

The 'underclass'

> The underclass *spawns* illegitimate children without a care for tomorrow and *feeds* on a crime rate which rivals the United States in property offences. Its able-bodied youths see no point in working and feel no compulsion either. They reject society while *feeding* off it; they are becoming a lost generation giving the cycle of deprivation a new spin . . . No amount of income redistribution or social engineering can solve their problem. Their *sub*-lifestyles

'Restaurant owners on the Strand plan to flood out, like so much rubbish, homeless young people who have had to make the pavements their home.'

are beyond welfare benefit rises and job creation schemes. They exist as active social outcasts, wedded to an anti-social system.'

(*Sunday Times* Editorial – our emphasis)[22]

These days the word 'underclass' is on everyone's lips. A broad cross-section of leader writers, academics, and journalists seem to share the belief that Britain is characterised by the growth of an 'underclass' which is cut off from the rest of society.[23] The concept has its roots in the United States where its chief exponent is political scientist Charles Murray.[24] In an article in the *Sunday Times*, Murray defined the characteristics of the 'underclass': high rates of illegitimacy, of crime and drop-out from the labour market. Thus the term 'underclass' describes a type of poverty that is defined by *behaviour*:

> When I use the term 'underclass' I am indeed focusing on a certain type of poor person defined not by his condition – eg, long-term unemployed – but by his *deplorable behaviour in response to that condition* – eg, unwilling to take the jobs that are available to him.[26]   (our emphasis)

From the point of view of their exponents, both 'dependency' and 'underclass' appeal because they create a distinction between different groups of people in poverty. A new lease of life is given to the old distinction between the deserving and undeserving poor. For example, Digby Anderson, director of the Social Affairs Unit, argues:[27]

> A more common sense morality would distinguish between those in difficulty through no fault of their own . . . and those who contributed to their circumstances. For, increasingly, low incomes are associated with behaviour, such as irresponsible sexual habits and unstable family formation, lack of commitment to work or training and failure to save or to spend prudently . . . It is time to bring back the notions of deserving and undeserving poor, to restore moral discrimination to social policy.

For Murray and others, the solution to the problem of the 'underclass' is not money, or training, or education. Instead, they suggest that the answer lies in a radical dose of 'self-government', whereby the views of local communities determine welfare policy. Digby Anderson presents the case rather more starkly than most by arguing for the return of social stigma:[28]

> The fundamental dispute is whether the welfare of a society including the poor may need the disincentives, stigma and other unpleasantnesses which arise naturally in local communities to dissuade people from poverty-producing behaviour.

By contrast, commentators like Frank Field MP have used the term 'underclass' in quite a different way.[29] For Field, the creation of such a class is primarily the consequence of structural factors and in his terms comprises the long-term unemployed, single parents and elderly people who are dependent solely on state benefits. He sees the 'underclass' as excluded from the rights of citizenship, separated from the rest of society in terms of 'income, life chances and aspirations'. He believes that, alongside other measures, policies on maintenance, pensions and availability for work will help to reduce its numbers.

So what is objectionable about the use of the term 'underclass'? Firstly, it is imprecise. Murray has used it to describe behaviour. Others, such as Frank Field, have placed the 'underclass' in the context of social and economic trends. It is not clear whether the 'underclass' describes all the poor, or sub-groups of the poor. If the latter, precisely which sub-groups fall into this category and why? Are they defined by their economic status or their 'deviance' from the norm? In short there is no clear evidence that such a class exists:

> At a time when British poverty is again being discussed in terms of an underclass, it is of crucial importance to recognise that these families and probably millions more like them living on social security benefits, are in no sense a detached and isolated group cut off from the rest of society. They are just the same people as the rest of our population, with the same culture and aspirations but with simply too little money to be able to share in the activities and possessions of everyday life with the rest of the population.
>
> (*Living on the Edge*)[30]

Secondly, the concept of an 'underclass' allows poverty to be explained away by personal and moral considerations, while allowing social and economic factors to be conveniently overshadowed. This is not to suggest that people's behaviour does not matter, but that poverty cannot be explained solely in terms of that behaviour since to do so is to abdicate collective responsibility for change. Interestingly Murray is not concerned with the behaviour of the rich. As Bob Holman writes:[31]

> Murray has no blame for the behaviour of the rich. Cabinet ministers who beget children outside marriage, Oxbridge students who use drugs, stockbrokers who commit fraud, the London Docklands affluent who . . . build security fences to make themselves a separate group, do not lead Mr Murray to write an attack on the 'overclass'. By just blaming the poor, he is making them victims.

As commentators refer to the 'underclass' with greater frequency, public opinion is moving in the opposite direction. A survey of attitudes to poverty in Europe found that in 1989 people in Britain were far more likely to believe that poverty is caused by injustice, rather than personal fault, than they did in the middle seventies (see p124). [32]

Thirdly, the term 'underclass' is heavy with negative resonance. It brings to mind the underworld, the sub-human, the underbelly of society, the wayward, drunken, feckless, 'dangerous' classes that the Victorians inveighed against. The quotation from the *Sunday Times* (see pp12-14) describes the 'underclass' as though it were a parasite, spawning offspring, and feeding off the rest of society. Thus, the term expresses more about the *fears* of the rest of society than about the reality it seeks to describe. As Ruth Lister has suggested: [33]

> The danger is that the more certain groups in poverty are described in such value-laden language, the easier it becomes for the rest of society to write them off as beyond the bonds of common citizenship.

Conclusion

We have challenged the view that 'real' poverty has been solved by a prosperous economy. Absolute poverty cannot be relegated to the annals of history with a sweep of the hand – people still do not have enough to eat or adequate clothing or a roof over their heads. But we have also argued that it is crucial to look at poverty in relation to the living standards of the rest of society. To do without the things that the rest of society regards as essential – a fridge, toys for the children, being able to give a birthday present – is to experience real poverty. We have disputed the idea of a 'dependency culture', arguing that dependency is part of the human condition; and we have argued that the concept of an 'underclass' responsible for its poverty by virtue of its own behaviour cannot be sustained. The pages which follow concentrate on the facts about, and causes of, poverty. They show that despite society's prosperity, the number of people living in poverty has increased and that this poverty is the outcome not of inadequacy but of broader social and economic factors.

NOTES

1. *Faith in the City*, Church House, 1985.
2. Quoted in J Veit Wilson, 'Paradigms of poverty', *Journal of Social Policy*, January 1986.
3. K Joseph, *Stranded on middle ground*, Centre for Policy Studies, 1976.
4. *Faith in the City*, Church House, 1985.
5. Adam Smith, *The Wealth of Nations*, 1812.
6. P Townsend, *Poverty in the UK*, Penguin, 1979.
7. See debate between David Piachaud and Peter Townsend in *New Society*, 10 and 18 September 1981.
8. House of Commons, 6 November 1979.
9. S McEvaddy and C Oppenheim, 'Christmas on the breadline', CPAG Ltd, 1987.
10. J Mack and S Lansley, *Poor Britain*, Allen & Unwin, 1985. This work is currently being updated.
11. 'Fair Shares?', CPAG video, 1984.
12. Speech by Rt Hon John Moore MP, on 'The end of the line for poverty', 11 May 1989.
13. K Joseph, quoted in K Hoover and R Plant, *Conservative capitalism in Britain and the United States: a critical appraisal*, Routledge, 1989.
14. DSS, *Households below Average Income*, Government Statistical Service, 1990.
15. Letter from the Prime Minister, Rt Hon Margaret Thatcher MP, to Rt Hon Neil Kinnock MP, 30 May 1989.
16. Speech by Rt Hon John Moore MP, on 'The future of the welfare state', 26 September 1987.
17. Letter from Rt Hon Nicholas Scott MP, Minister of State for Social Security and Disabled People, to Peter Barclay CBE, Chair of the Social Security Advisory Committee, 25 August 1987.
18. *Crossbow*, Autumn 1988.
19. Quoted in 'The impact of social security changes: the views of families using Barnardos pre-school services', G Craig and C Glendinning, Barnardos Research and Development, 1990.
20. *see* note 19.
21. R Plant, 'The New Right and social policy: a critique', in *Social Policy Review 1989-1990*, Longman, 1990.
22. *Sunday Times*, 26 November 1989.
23. See C Oppenheim in *Social Work Today*, 26 October 1989.
24. The full exposition of some of Murray's views can be found in C Murray, *Losing ground*, Basic Books Inc (USA), 1984.
25. *Sunday Times*, 26 November 1989.
26. C Murray, 'Rejoinder', *The emerging British underclass*, Institute for Economic Affairs, 1990.
27. D Anderson, *Sunday Times*, 29 July 1990.
28. D Anderson, *Sunday Times*, 20 May 1990.
29. F Field, *Losing out: the emergence of Britain's underclass*, Blackwell, 1989.
30. J Bradshaw and H Holmes, *Living on the edge: a study of the living standards of families on benefit in Tyne & Wear*, Tyneside CPAG, 1989.
31. B Holman, *Social Work Today*, 16 August 1990.
32. 'The perception of poverty in Europe', *Eurobarometer*, Commission of the European Communities, 1990.
33. R Lister, *The exclusive society: citizenship and the poor*, CPAG Ltd, 1990.

TWO

Poverty: the facts

CPAG is in no doubt about the existence, growth and nature of poverty in the United Kingdom today. At its heart, poverty is about exclusion from social participation. However, unlike other countries – such as the United States – in the United Kingdom there is no official poverty line, no government sanctioned marker which admits the existence of poverty. Nevertheless, since our task is to estimate the extent of poverty, we need to establish such a line – one which divides those who are poor from those who are not poor.

We have chosen to look at two possible poverty lines. Both are derived from the same source – the *Family Expenditure Survey*, an annual government survey of around 7,000 private households which monitors both incomes and expenditure. Each approach has its strengths and weaknesses, and by examining the two side by side we are able to present a more rounded picture of poverty for the years 1979-87.

The first poverty line is based on the *Low Income Families* (LIF)[1] statistics which were originally published by the DSS (for the years 1972-1985) and subsequently by the independent Institute for Fiscal Studies.[2] This series shows the numbers of people living on, below or just above the old supplementary benefit level. CPAG uses supplementary benefit as a proxy for the poverty line.

The second poverty line is based on *Households below Average Income*[3] statistics with which the government replaced LIF. We use 50% of average income – the lowest level of income measured by the government's statistics – as a proxy for the poverty line.

In addition, we also take account of those people living just above each of these poverty lines – those living on the margins of poverty. It is important to hold on to the idea of such a margin, since people living on low incomes usually find that their income fluctuates, slipping between poverty and an income close to poverty. We describe anyone living between 100% and 140% of supplementary benefit or between 50% and 60% of average income as living on the margins of poverty.

As we shall see, despite their different approaches what both methods reveal is crystal clear – that the income represented by either poverty line is unacceptably low in an affluent and civilised society. Living on such levels of income excludes people from the basic goods, resources and services which they have a right to expect. The statistics demonstrate that:

- In 1987, 2,890,000 people (5% of the population) were living *below* supplementary benefit level. In 1979, 4% of the population were living below the supplementary benefit level.
- In 1987, 10,200,000 people (around 19% of the population) were living on or below the supplementary benefit level. In 1979, 6% of the population were living on or below the supplementary benefit level.
- In 1987, 10,500,000 people (around 19% of the population) were living below 50% of average income. In 1979, 9% of the population were living below 50% of average income.
- Between 1979 and 1987 the poorest tenth of the population saw their incomes rise by just 0.1% in real terms (after housing costs), while the average rose by 23%.

So, whichever way you measure it, poverty has grown significantly over recent years and by 1987 over 10 million people in Britain – close to a fifth of our society – were living in poverty.

What is the context in which we are looking at the changes in poverty? The figures from both series cover the period 1979 to 1987. During that time there were major economic and social changes. They included:

- the tripling of unemployment to a peak of over three million in 1986, followed by a small drop in the latter part of 1987;[4]
- very substantial rises in average incomes – a rise of around 117% in personal disposable income over the period in cash terms;[5]
- inflation increased by 82% over the period 1979-87 (with a peak of 22% in 1980); inflation for the low paid grew faster than for the rest of the population;[6]
- a small rise in the percentage of single parents;[7]
- some contributory parts of the social security system such as unemployment benefit were weakened, leaving many more people to fall back on means-tested supplementary benefit;
- employment patterns gradually changed, with part-time labour playing an increasingly important role in the development of industrial strategy;
- reductions in income tax brought bonuses for the average earner, but windfalls for the rich.

In short, the persistence of high unemployment coupled with increased average earnings forged a much wider gap between the people who were dependent solely on benefits (which generally rise by the level of inflation only) or reliant on low wages and the people on average earnings and above.

What the figures miss out

Both *Low Income Families* and *Households below Average Income exclude* the following from their figures:
- a breakdown by ethnic origin
- a breakdown by sex
- a distinction between part-time and full-time workers (which is becoming more important as employment patterns change – see Chapter 4)
- people living in institutions – eg, hospitals, nursing homes, residential care homes and prisons
- homeless people

The exclusion of homeless people and people living in institutions means that *all* the figures we present below are likely to be an *underestimate*. This is because homeless people and many people living in institutions usually have very little money.

The first source: Low Income Families statistics

What are the Low Income Families statistics?

For many years supplementary benefit was widely used as a proxy for a poverty line. Income support replaced supplementary benefit in 1988 as part of the overall social security changes. (It has a different structure from its predecessor – instead of the scale rates and extra weekly payments for certain needs in SB, there are personal allowances and premiums for certain groups such as pensioners, families with children, single parents, and people with disabilities.) Supplementary benefit/ income support is a means-tested social security benefit – often known as the safety-net. It is set each year by Parliament as a minimum level of income for people who are not in full-time work who meet certain conditions. *Low Income Families* (LIF) shows the numbers of people living below 140% of supplementary benefit. CPAG argued that people living on and below supplementary benefit were living in poverty and that people living between 100% and 140% of supplementary benefit were living on the margins of poverty. The DSS defined up to 140% of supplementary benefit as low income.

What is the poverty line in the Low Income Families statistics?

The poverty line is measured by the level of supplementary benefit. It shows that in 1987 a two-parent family with 2 children below 11 years of age were living in poverty if they had an income (after paying for their

---

TABLE 1

The poverty line in 1987/88 and in 1990/91 using supplementary benefit (SB) / income support (after housing costs)

Family type	1987/88 Supplementary benefit scale rates	1990/91 Income support personal allowances
Pensioners		
Single person	£38.65	£48.50
Couple	£61.85	£75.55
Non pensioners		
Single person	£24.35 (non householder rate)	£28.80 (18-24 rate)
	£30.40 (householder rate)	£36.70 (25 + rate)
Single person with		
1 child aged under 11	£40.80	£60.50
Couple	£49.35	£57.60
Couple with 2 children		
(aged under 11)	£70.15	£89.65

Note:
1. *These figures are the levels of benefit that were paid at the time (ie, they are cash figures which are not adjusted for inflation).*
2. *LIF uses the* long-term rate *of supplementary benefit as the threshold to measure pensioners' incomes. In all other cases the short-term rate is used.*
3. *LIF also includes an automatic addition of £2.20 for children aged under 5 and of £1.20 for pensioners (£2.20 less £1 available scale margin).*
SOURCE: National Welfare Benefits Handbook 1987/88 and 1990/91, CPAG Ltd, 1987 and 1990

housing costs) of £70.15 a week. If the level of IS is used as the rough equivalent of the poverty line today, it shows that in 1990 the same type of family were living in poverty if they had an income (after housing costs) of £89.65 a week. In Table 1 we show what the poverty line is for different families using supplementary benefit/income support to define poverty.

What do the figures from Low Income Families statistics show?

The *Low Income Families* statistics show that in 1987 in Great Britain[8]:
- 10,200,000 people – close to a fifth (19%) of the population – were living in poverty (on or below supplementary benefit level). Of these, 2,890,000 people – 5% of the population – were living *below* the poverty line;
- a total of 15,360,000 people – 28% of the population – were living in or on the margins of poverty (up to 140% of the supplementary benefit level).

Figure 1 shows the rises in the numbers of people living in poverty or on

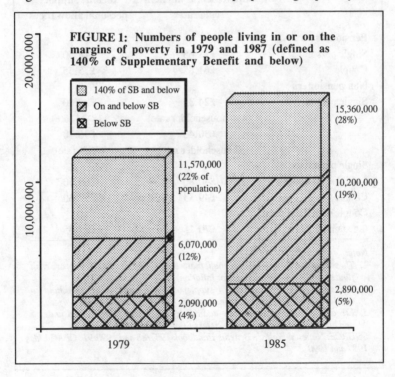

FIGURE 1: Numbers of people living in or on the margins of poverty in 1979 and 1987 (defined as 140% of Supplementary Benefit and below)

140% of SB and below
On and below SB
Below SB

11,570,000 (22% of population)
6,070,000 (12%)
2,090,000 (4%)

15,360,000 (28%)
10,200,000 (19%)
2,890,000 (5%)

1979   1985

its margins between 1979 and 1987. Although there is a slight discontinuity between the figures, it is nevertheless possible to identify the broad trends[9]. In 1979, 12% of the population were living in poverty (on or below supplementary benefit); by 1987 this had risen to 19%.

The Institute for Fiscal Studies suggest that two-thirds of the increase between 1979 and 1987 in the numbers on supplementary benefit is due to the rise in unemployment. The decline in the value of unemployment benefit also pushed a growing number of people on to supplementary benefit (see p66). They note that there has not been such a large increase in the numbers living below and just above supplementary benefit. Part of the rise in the numbers living in poverty defined this way is due to a small rise in the real level of supplementary benefit. (However, it is important to bear in mind that people on low income have different spending patterns, spending more on food, housing and fuel as a proportion of their overall spending. Between 1979 and 1987 inflation measured by the low-paid price index, which reflects these different spending patterns, was higher than the ordinary rise in inflation. [10] Real rises in supplementary benefit over this period therefore have to be put into context.) Moreover, as the Institute points out, average earnings rose much faster than inflation, leaving the poorest way behind the rest of the population:

> It is immediately clear that while the real value of the supplementary benefit scale rates actually increased a little over the period, average earnings increased much faster. This implies that as well as the numbers on and around the supplementary benefit line having increased considerably, the level of income represented by that line has fallen significantly in relation to average earnings. Thus, although people appearing in the tables in 1987 were no worse off than those appearing in 1979, they were much further behind the rest of the population. *(Low Income Families, 1979-1987)* [11]

How many children?

> It is such a pathetic look on her face when she notices the toys have been broken and repaired. Is this all there is to living on supplementary benefit?
> (Mother of three, Carryduff) [12]

In 1987: [13]

- there were 2,490,000 children – 21% of all children – living in poverty (on or below the supplementary benefit level). Of these 490,000 (4% of all children) were living below the poverty line. In 1979 there were 1,180,000 children living in poverty (9%); of these 290,000 (2%) were living below the poverty line;
- there were 3,610,000 children – 30% of all children – living in or

on the margins of poverty (below 140% of supplementary benefit). In 1979 2,370,000 children were living in or on the margins of poverty (18%).

This is an appropriate point to examine two additional aspects of the facts and figures relating to poverty. Firstly, we can look at the total *number* in poverty and break this down into groups. Secondly, we can look at the *risk* certain groups of the population have of falling into poverty.

In 1987, 1.1 million children living in poverty were growing up in a single parent family – 45% of all children in poverty. The risk of poverty for children in single parent families is very high – 70% of children growing up in single parent families were living in poverty compared to 13% in two parent families. Table 2 describes the number of children living in or on the margins of poverty by family type:

TABLE 2

Children in or on the margins of poverty (defined as 140% of supplementary benefit and below) by family type in 1987

	Children in couples	Children in one parent families
Below SB	440,000	50,000
	(4%)	(3%)
On and below SB	1,380,000	1,110,000
	(13%)	(70%)
Below 140% of SB	2,400,000	1,210,000
	(23%)	(76%)

Note: Figures in brackets are the proportion of children in two-parent and single parent families living below various income levels.

Falling through the safety-net

One of the most important things that the LIF figures reveal is how many people fall through the safety-net of supplementary benefit. [14] Who are they and why? In 1987, there were a total of 1,910,000 families and 2,890,000 people who were living on incomes below the state minimum. The groups who were most vulnerable to falling through the safety-net were couples with children and single people without children (the former made up 31% of the total who were living below supplementary benefit and the latter 26% – see *fig* 2). Looking at *non-pensioners* living below supplementary benefit (who numbered 1,960,000) 48% were in full-time work or self-employed, 46% were unemployed and 5% were

TABLE 3

Reasons for families falling below the poverty line (supplementary benefit) in 1987

		Proportion of total below supplementary benefit
Total	1,910,000	
Full time workers	170,000	9%
of which:		
families with children	90,000	5%
Self-employed	200,000	11%
Income above capital limit	310,000	16%
Young dependants*	300,000	16%
Families taken below supplementary benefit because of their housing costs	130,000	7%
Non-take-up of means-tested benefit	810,000	42%
of which:		
housing benefit supplement	320,000	17%
housing benefit	200,000	11%
supplementary benefit	290,000	15%

Note: percentages do not add up exactly to 100% because of rounding.
* *These people are almost exclusively young single people under 25 years of age living with their parents.*

The Institute for Fiscal Studies extends the government's LIF surveys by looking at why people fall below the supplementary benefit line. [15] They found that the average (median) income of those below that line was around three-quarters (74%) of supplementary benefit. These figures have to be treated with caution because they are very sensitive to assumptions about housing costs. What they demonstrate is that not taking up the benefit to which a family is entitled is an important cause of poverty – 42% of those who fell through the safety-net were *not claiming a means-tested benefit to which they were entitled*. Table 3 shows the reasons for families (note these figures are for families, *not* persons within families) falling below supplementary benefit.

FIGURE 2:
Numbers living below the poverty line (Supplementary Benefit)
in 1987 by family type
NOTE: Percentages do not add up to 100% due to rounding

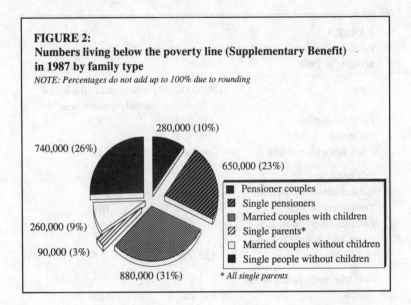

280,000 (10%)

740,000 (26%)

650,000 (23%)

260,000 (9%)

90,000 (3%)

880,000 (31%)

- ■ Pensioner couples
- ▨ Single pensioners
- ▒ Married couples with children
- ▨ Single parents*
- □ Married couples without children
- ■ Single people without children

* All single parents

The second source: Households below Average Income

What are the Households below Average Income statistics?

Households below Average Income was published for the first time in 1988. [16] It is now the major source of official information about people living on a low income. The latest edition, *Households below Average Income 1981-1987*, was issued quietly in the summer of 1990 just before MPs went off on their summer holidays. (Interestingly, the series actually contains data from 1979 which are omitted from the title and relegated to an annex at the back.) It examines the living standards of people in the lower half of the income distribution. The series shows:

- the number of individuals in households with incomes below various thresholds, from 50% average household income to average household income;
- the number of individuals living in households in the bottom 10%, 20%, 30%, 40% and 50% of the income distribution (these are known as decile groups), and the rises in real income for each of these groups.

What is the poverty line in Households below Average Income?

Households below Average Income (HBAI) does not contain an obvious poverty line. It is not possible to use the poorest 10% of the population as a poverty line as this group does not change over time (10% of the population will always be 10%). Press reports of the figures generally cited the lowest measure of income – 50% of average income – as a poverty line. This is the definition frequently used in the European Community – 50% of average national income marks the poverty line.

HBAI presents figures both before and after housing costs. There are arguments for using both measures. [17] We have chosen in most cases here to use figures which show numbers and income after housing costs for the following reasons: firstly, the figures are more comparable with supplementary benefit/income support (as these are also after housing costs); secondly, housing expenditure is different from other kinds of expenditure – it varies widely depending on the area in which you live, and the time in your life; and thirdly, it is also a fixed cost for many families, particularly those on low incomes, who often have little choice about the amount they spend on their housing and therefore about the money they have left, for example, to spend on their children's needs.

What is half the average income in cash terms?
Using HBAI we show in Table 4 what a poverty line measured by 50% of average income was in 1987 (the date of the latest set of figures) and updated to 1990 for different types of family. To update the figures to 1990 we have raised the 1987 figures in line with the rise in personal disposable income per head (a rise of 31%). [18] In 1987 a two parent family with 2 children (aged 3 and 6) on an income of less than £102 a week (after paying for their housing costs) was living below the poverty line (defined as below 50% of average income). In 1990 a similar family with an income of less than £134 a week was living below the poverty line defined in the same way.

What do the figures show in Households below Average Income?

Households below Average Income (HBAI) are the official figures on low income. These figures are different from the figures in LIF (see p42-3 for a discussion of how they compare). HBAI shows that in Great Britain in 1987 (see *fig* 3) [19]:

- 10,500,000 people were living in poverty (below 50% of average income) – 19%, or nearly a fifth, of the population. This is nearly double the number in 1979 – 4,930,000 – 9% of the population.
- 16,150,000 were living in or on the margins of poverty (below

TABLE 4   The poverty line in 1987 and 1990: defined as 50% average income (after housing costs) £ per week

	1987	1990
	50% of average income £ per week	
single person	£40	£52
couple	£73	£96
single person with 1 child (aged 3)	£53	£69
couple with 2 children (aged 3 and 6)	£102	£134

Notes:
1. *Figures for 1990 are based on uprating the figures for 1987 by the rise in personal disposable income per head between 1987 and 1990.*
2. *These figures are cash figures which are not adjusted for inflation.*
3. *The figures are based on the average equivalised income in 1987 of £145 a week. This is then halved and unequivalised for different family types using the equivalence scales in HBAI (see definitions and terms).*
SOURCE: Letter from Department of Social Security to CPAG, 3.9.90.

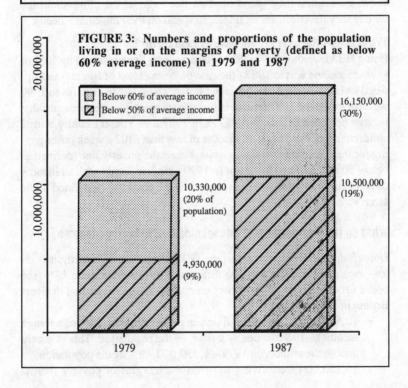

FIGURE 3: Numbers and proportions of the population living in or on the margins of poverty (defined as below 60% average income) in 1979 and 1987

Below 60% of average income
Below 50% of average income

16,150,000 (30%)

10,330,000 (20% of population)

10,500,000 (19%)

4,930,000 (9%)

1979   1987

60% of average income) – 30%, or nearly a third, of the population. This compares to 10,330,000 – 20% of the population – in 1979 measured in this way.

Who is in poverty?

It is the *unemployed, low paid and pensioners* who account for most of the people living in poverty. Of the 10,500,000 living in poverty in 1987 (defined as below 50% average income): [20]

- 22% were pensioners – 2,330,000
- 26% were in full-time work – 2,680,000
- 5% were people with a sickness or disability – 500,000
- 11% were single parents – 1,150,000 (single parents in this group are those who were not working full time)
- 28% were unemployed – 2,910,000
- 9% fell into the group 'others' – 910,000. ('Others' consisted of men aged 60-64, widows, students, people temporarily away from work, carers and people who are unemployed but not available for work)

(**Note:** Figures do not add up exactly to 10,500,000 and percentages do not add up exactly to 100 because of rounding.)

The chances of falling into poverty were much higher for certain groups of people: 6 out of every 10 unemployed people and single parents (who were not working full time) were living in poverty (see *fig* 4).

Another main cause of poverty is the inability of people's incomes to meet their familial responsibilities. [21] In 1987 5,590,000 people in *families with children* were living in poverty (defined as below 50% of average income), making up over half (53%) of all those in poverty.

Of the 10,500,000 living in poverty (below 50% of average income):

- 13% were married pensioners – 1,340,000;
- 10% were single pensioners – 1,000,000;
- 41% were married couples with children – 4,350,000;
- 9% were married couples without children – 970,000;
- 12% were single parents – 1,240,000 (this figure differs from the one above because it includes *all* single parents whether in full-time work or not);
- 16% were single people without children – 1,630,000;

(See note above.)

[My son] sleeps on a mattress and so do I. The baby hasn't got a cot. We've only got two chairs, there's no carpets or proper curtains and we haven't got a three piece suite.   (Mary, single mother of two) [22]

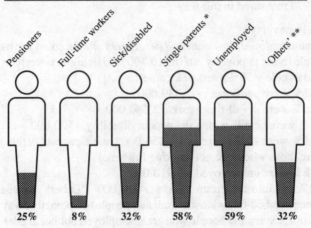

FIGURE 4: The risk of poverty by economic status in 1987

Pensioners Full-time workers Sick/disabled Single parents* Unemployed 'Others'**

25%   8%   32%   58%   59%   32%

Proportion living in poverty
(below 50% average income after housing costs)

* Single parents who are not in full-time work. **Men aged 60-64, widows, students, people
temporarily away from work, carers, people who are unemployed but not available for work

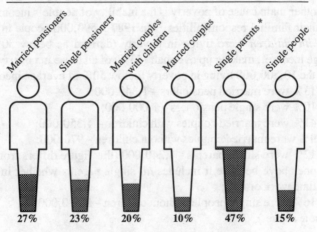

FIGURE 5: The risk of poverty by family status in 1987

Married pensioners Single pensioners Married couples with children Married couples Single parents* Single people

27%   23%   20%   10%   47%   15%

Proportion living in poverty
(below 50% average income after housing costs)

* All single parents

The risks of falling into poverty were higher for people with children than those who had no children and were particularly high for single parents. For all single parents – whether in or out of work – nearly half were living in poverty in 1987 (below 50% of average income) (see *fig* 5).

How many children?

> I just wish we had a little bit more so our children could have what other children have.
>
> (Mother of three, Northamptonshire)[23]

Poverty that afflicts children is perhaps the most shocking. The figures below show that children have been more vulnerable to poverty than society as a whole throughout the period from 1979 to 1987 (see *fig* 6).

In 1987, a higher proportion of children were living in poverty (defined as below 50% of average income) than the population as a whole:[24]

- there were 3,090,000 children living in poverty (defined as below 50% average income) – over a quarter (26%) of all children. This compares to 1,620,000 in 1979 – 12% of all children.

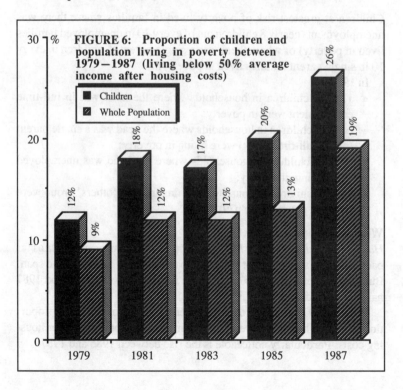

FIGURE 6: Proportion of children and population living in poverty between 1979–1987 (living below 50% average income after housing costs)

- there were 4,350,000 children living in or on the margins of poverty (defined as below 60% of average income) – over a third (36%) of all children. This compares with 3,030,000 – 23% – in 1979.

Which children are in poverty?
Of the 3,090,000 children living in poverty in 1987 (below 50% of average income): [25]
- 38% – 1,180,000 – were living in households where the head was in full-time work;
- 25% – 730,000 – were living in households where the head was a single parent (not in full-time work);
- 31% – 960,000 – were living in households where the head was unemployed;
- 8% – 240,000 – were living in households were the head was a pensioner, sick or disabled or fell into the 'others' category (see p29).

(**Note:** Figures do not all add up exactly to 3,090,000 and percentages do not add up exactly to 100 because of rounding.)

Children at greatest risk of poverty lived in families where there was unemployment (nearly 8 children out of every 10 in unemployed families lived in poverty) or where there was a single parent (6 children in every 10 in single parent families lived in poverty).
    In 1987:
- 13% of children in households where the head was in full-time employment were in poverty;
- 60% of children in households where the head was a single parent (not in full-time work) were living in poverty;
- 79% of children in households where the head was unemployed were living in poverty;
- 46% of children in households falling into the 'others' group were living in poverty (see p29).

What has happened since 1979?
Households below Average Income only provides comparative data as far back as 1979, so we cannot make comparisons over a longer time span. But poverty defined as 50% of average income between 1979 and 1987 has increased dramatically. [26]
    Between 1979 and 1987 there has been a substantial rise in the proportion of people living in poverty, whether measured before or after housing costs. Particularly noticeable is the rise between 1985 and 1987:

TABLE 5
Proportion and numbers living in poverty (below 50% of average income) both before and after housing costs

	Before housing costs		After housing costs	
	%	No: million	%	No: million
1979	7.1	3.75	9.4	4.93
1981	8.2	4.39	11.9	6.37
1983	8.0	4.28	11.5	6.21
1985	9.2	4.99	13.4	7.23
1987	14.3	7.72	19.4	10.50

SOURCE: AB Atkinson, DSS Report on Households below Average Income 1981-87, paper for the Social Services Select Committee, 1990

By looking at the poorest 10% of the population in 1979 and in 1987, we can see how the *composition* of the poorest groups has changed (after housing costs). [27] Figure 7 shows how pensioners made up a smaller proportion of the poorest 10% in 1987 than in 1979 (down from 26% to 12% of the bottom 10%); couples with children made up a larger proportion (up from 44% to 50%); and in particular single people without children leapt from making up 9% of the bottom 10% in 1979 to 19% in 1987 (largely due to higher unemployment). Looking at *economic* status, unemployment is directly apparent – in 1979 only 19% of the bottom 10% were unemployed, but by 1987 the figure had risen to a staggering 42%. Even the proportion of people in full-time work in the bottom 10% increased by a percentage point, despite the fact that average earnings over the period had risen substantially (see *fig* 8).

Growing divisions
The figures also show a stark picture of poor people falling further and further behind the rest of society since 1979. Between 1979 and 1987 the poorest 10% (known as decile group – see Definitions and Terms) experienced virtually no rise at all in their real income after housing costs, while the average had an increase of 23% (see Table 6). [28] Incomes before housing costs still show a very large gap between the poorest and the average – the incomes of the average rose by almost three times that of the poorest 10%. Even worse, between 1985 and 1987 the poorest 10% of the population experienced a *drop* in their real incomes after housing costs of 1.7%.

The people who were in the bottom 10% in 1987 are not necessarily

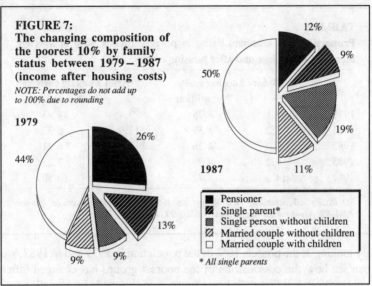

FIGURE 7:
The changing composition of
the poorest 10% by family
status between 1979 – 1987
(income after housing costs)
*NOTE: Percentages do not add up
to 100% due to rounding*

1979

26%

44%

13%

9%   9%

12%

9%

50%

19%

1987   11%

■ Pensioner
▨ Single parent*
▦ Single person without children
▧ Married couple without children
□ Married couple with children

* All single parents

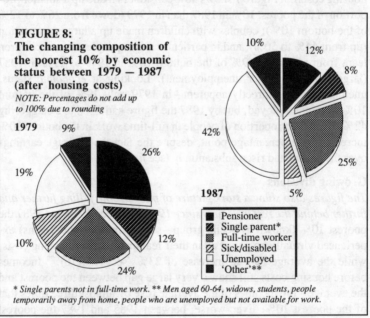

FIGURE 8:
The changing composition of
the poorest 10% by economic
status between 1979 — 1987
(after housing costs)
*NOTE: Percentages do not add up
to 100% due to rounding*

1979

26%

9%

19%

10%

12%

24%

10%

12%

8%

42%

25%

1987   5%

■ Pensioner
▨ Single parent*
▦ Full-time worker
▧ Sick/disabled
□ Unemployed
▦ 'Other'**

** Single parents not in full-time work. ** Men aged 60-64, widows, students, people
temporarily away from home, people who are unemployed but not available for work.*

TABLE 6
Percentage rises in real income by decile group between 1979 and 1987 (before and after housing costs)

	before housing costs	after housing costs
Bottom tenth	8.5%	0.1%
Second lowest tenth	6.8%	2.4%
Third lowest tenth	8.6%	2.8%
Fourth lowest tenth	10.6%	7.9%
Fifth lowest tenth	13.1%	11.9%
average	22.9%	23.1%

Note: The groups are not cumulative in this table. The mid-point (median – see Definitions and Terms) of each tenth is used here

the same people who were in the bottom 10% in 1979. However, as Tony Atkinson writes: [29]

> The figures do not mean that any one person has stayed in the (bottom tenth) since 1979 with the same real income. But if the person at this point in 1979 has moved up, then someone else has had a *fall* in real income.

Poor people have found that their share of total income after housing costs has fallen between 1979 and 1987. The share of the bottom 10% fell from 3.9% to 3.0%, and the share of the bottom 50% fell from nearly a third (32.2%) to just over a quarter (27.5%) (see Table 7). [30] Meanwhile, the richest 50% increased their share of total income from just over two-thirds (67.8%) to close to three-quarters (72.5%) between 1979 and 1987. As Atkinson explains: [31]

> The Report No 7 of the Royal Commission on the Distribution of Income and Wealth found that the income share of the bottom half of the population was little different in 1976-77 from that in 1949, concluding that 'the income distribution shows remarkable stability from year to year.'

We are witnessing the reversal of a long-term pattern. The share of income of the poorer sections of society is shrinking for the first time since the Second World War.

The contribution of social security benefits
The clearest indicator of the increased significance of the means-test is that by 1987 1 in 4 of the population were reliant on a means-tested benefit. Not surprisingly, the poorest 10% of the population are very

TABLE 7
Share of total income after housing costs broken down into decile groups in 1979 and 1987

	1979	1987
Bottom 10%	3.9%	3.0%
Bottom 20%	9.5%	7.6%
Bottom 30%	16.0%	13.1%
Bottom 40%	23.6%	19.7%
Bottom 50%	32.2%	27.5%
Top 50%	67.8%	72.5%

dependent on social security benefits for their income. In 1987, 63% of the poorest 10% received supplementary benefit or housing benefit, in comparison with 24% for the population as a whole.[32] This is a substantial rise in comparison with 1979, when 52% of the bottom 10% and 17% of the population as a whole received supplementary or housing benefit.

Benefits made a crucial contribution to the incomes of the poorest. In 1987, 70% of the income of the poorest 10% came from social security benefits, compared with just 17% for the population as a whole (see Table 8).[33] This illustrates the importance of raising benefits at least in line with inflation. In addition, it shows that if benefits are allowed to decline in relation to other incomes the poorest fall further and further behind. The freeze of child benefit is a case in point:

> My husband is on a small wage. I rely every week on child benefit to buy food for my three children, my husband and myself. It is not a fringe benefit for us, it is an absolute essential as I never receive any housekeeping from my husband; all his wages go on the mortgage repayment, gas, electricity bills etc.
>
> ('Dear Mr Moore, Letters from parents about Child Benefit')[34]

Table 8 shows the importance of child benefit which contributes 11% to the incomes of the bottom 10%.[35] Compare this with means-tested support for low-paid families – family income supplement (FIS) which, because of restricted eligibility and low take-up rates, fails to appear in Table 8 at all. (Averaging over the whole series, FIS only contributed 2% or less to the incomes of the bottom 10%.) Although the more generous family credit has replaced FIS, the take-up rate has remained low (see p72).

TABLE 8
The percentage contribution of social security to the incomes of the poorest 10% and the population as a whole in 1987

	Poorest 10%	Total Population
Means-tested benefits:	38%	5.1%
supplementary benefit	27%	2.9%
housing benefit	10%	2.1%
Other (eg, family income supplement)	1%	0.1%
Non-means-tested benefits:	32%	11.5%
retirement pension	14%	5.7%
child benefit	11%	2.7%
Total from social security	70%	16.6%
Other sources (such as earnings and savings)	30%	83.4%

Note: income is before housing costs

The search for a poverty line

Measuring poverty is an exercise in demarcation. Lines have to be drawn where none may be visible and they have to be made bold. Where one draws the line is itself a battlefield.

(Megnad Desai, *Excluding the Poor*) [36]

We have looked at two sources of information to estimate the numbers living in poverty and the changes in their incomes. However, neither measure of poverty is entirely satisfactory.

The limitations of the statistics

Firstly, the statistics are snapshots – they do *not* show *how long* people are living in poverty for, it could be a week, months or even years. The people living on or below supplementary benefit or 50% of average income in 1987 may be entirely different people from those living on those levels of income in 1979 (see pp33-5). So the figures do not convey the intensity of poverty which results from spending a long time living on a low income.

Secondly, the statistics do not show the *depth* of poverty people experience – ie, how far below 50% of average income people fall. (In fact the analysis by the Institute for Fiscal Studies of LIF touches on this question by showing that the average income for people living below the supplementary benefit level was 74% of supplementary benefit. However, they do not look at the levels of income in great detail.)

And thirdly, any approach which uses income alone to measure poverty can only provide a partial picture. It does not convey the standard of living offered by such an income. For instance, the time taken to generate that income (eg, through long hours of low-paid work, see Chapter 6) or the costs of basic goods or services which have to met from that income. For example, in the switch from supplementary benefit to income support, changes were made in the costs which claimants had to meet from their basic benefit. Income support no longer meets payment for water rates and only covers 80% of the poll tax (supplementary benefit used to cover water rates and 100% of rates). Thus, using the benefit rate alone tells us nothing about the costs that people have to now meet from their benefit.

These are problems common to both our poverty lines. Below we look at the advantages and disadvantages of using either the supplementary benefit level or 50% of average income as a poverty line.

The advantages and disadvantages of using supplementary benefit as a poverty line

Advantages:
- Supplementary benefit is a minimum level of income set by Parliament for people not in full-time work who meet certain conditions. It allows us to measure incomes in relation to this minimum level and thus judge how effective the government is in ensuring that people do not fall below it and that they are given the resources to rise above it.
- LIF uses the 'family' (or the benefit assessment unit – see Definitions and Terms) as the unit of measurement rather than the 'household' (as is used by HBAI). More than one family may live in a single household. For example, if a single-parent family on supplementary benefit shares with a relative or friend who is on an average income, the single-parent family is still counted as having a low income despite the higher income of the relative or friend. This reflects the assumption that income is not always shared fairly within households. CPAG believes that the best unit of measure-

ment is the individual; but the 'family' is closer to the 'individual' unit than 'household'. Thus, on the whole the 'family' is a more appropriate unit of measurement than 'household'.

Disadvantages: [37]

- These are not official figures, but have been produced by the independent Institute for Fiscal Studies.
- The difficulty of using supplementary benefit both as a measure of poverty and as the tool to relieve poverty. Each time it is raised in real terms (ie, above inflation) to improve the living standards of the poorest, the number of people defined as poor is automatically increased. If supplementary benefit was reduced by half, the numbers living in poverty would also be halved.
- Supplementary benefit's level and coverage is determined by overall government priorities, rather than being related to people's needs. Thus, by using a benefit level as a poverty line, the anomalies in the benefit itself are mirrored in the way poverty is measured, eg, supplementary benefit was paid at two rates – short and long term. Pensioners, for example, were paid the long-term rate. LIF uses the long-term rate as the threshold for pensioners' incomes, but not for other types of families. This means that the poverty line was higher for pensioners than other groups of people, such as families with children.

The advantages and disadvantages of using 50% of average income as a poverty line

Advantages:

- These are official figures published by the government.
- It is an unapologetically 'relative' poverty line (see Chapter 1) which looks at low incomes in relation to the incomes of the rest of society. 50% of average income rises and falls as average income rises and falls.
- The definition of poverty used by the European Community is 50% of average national income, so 50% of average income in Britain would be a similar approach.

Disadvantages:

- 50% of average income does not relate incomes to the minimum rates of benefit specified by Parliament – supplementary benefit now income support. This means we can no longer judge the government by its own standards.

- The figures are based on the *household* unit rather than the *family* unit, as was used in the LIF figures (see p38). Using the *household* unit leads to a substantial *underestimate* of the number of people living on a low income. The Institute for Fiscal Studies estimated that by using *households* as the unit of measurement rather than *families* the new series could have underestimated the numbers living below 50% the average income in 1983 by as much as 1.5 million. [38]
- Some people would argue that 50% of average income measures inequality rather than poverty.
- The 'average' may fluctuate from year to year for either statistical reasons or economic ones. For example, if average income fell drastically, say as a result of an oil-shock induced recession, the number of people below 50% average income (and thus in 'poverty') would also fall even though many of those on low incomes may actually be worse off.

The list of advantages and disadvantages makes it abundantly clear that there is no straightforward answer to finding an uncontroversial poverty line. We have chosen to use both the LIF and HBAI, drawing out the strengths of each analysis.

Comparing the results

Comparing the poverty lines
How do the two measures of poverty compare?

Firstly *the level of income measured by both poverty lines is unacceptably low*. In 1987 a family with children under 11 living on supplementary benefit had just £1.50 a day to spend on each child's needs; in 1990 the same family on income support would have just £1.75 a day. [39]

The poverty line of 50% of average income is slightly higher than the income measured by supplementary benefit or income support. (In fact the average that is used in HBAI is the 'mean' – see Definitions and Terms – which tends to be dragged up by those people who have higher incomes. The 'median' tends to be a more stable average as it represents 'typical' income. Thus 50% of the mean is likely to be a higher figure than 50% of the median.)

- In 1987, 50% of average income ranged from about 104% to 164% of supplementary benefit rates for different types of families (using the short-term rate of supplementary benefit in all cases apart from pensioners).

- In 1990, 50% of average income ranged from about 107% to 181% of income support.

Between 1987 and 1990 there was an increase in the gap between 50% of average income and supplementary benefit and 50% of average income and income support. This is both the result of the substantial rise in average incomes over the period and the very low levels of benefit for some groups of income support claimants, in particular those who are not entitled to any premiums to top up their benefit (see Definitions and Terms). For example, in 1990 50% of average income for a single person with no children is £52 a week compared to £28.80 income support for a young person without children aged between 18 and 24 – ie, 50% of average income is 181% of income support. This is because average incomes for single people without children are high and the income support rate particularly low.

Does this mean that in 1987 using 50% of average income as a poverty line exaggerates the extent of poverty? Clearly not, since firstly, HBAI used 'household' income rather than 'family' income. Thus, the poverty line of 50% of average income derived from HBAI is likely to underestimate the extent of poverty (see p40). To some extent this offsets the fact that 50% of average income is higher than the poverty line measured by supplementary benefit. Secondly, if you compare 50% of average income with the long-term rate of supplementary benefit for all claimants the gap is much smaller. Thirdly, and most importantly, there is an overwhelming evidence to show that living on supplementary benefit means substantial hardship. Below we show what living on either poverty line means.

Living on the poverty line
We have identified the very low figures of income represented by either supplementary benefit or 50% of average income. What does it mean to live on these levels of income?

A retired senior Department of Social Security official wrote:

> It is hard for many, and impossible for some – particularly families with dependent children on the basic rates – to maintain reasonably decent standards for any appreciable length of time without help from other sources. For them, life on supplementary benefit is a bleak struggle to make ends meet.
>
> (G Beltram, *Testing the Safety Net*)[40]

An analysis of the average expenditure of families living on supplementary benefit in 1986 showed that a family with two children could expect to have a diet of 6,500 calories short of nutritional adequacy a week, and would have to make a coat last for 15 years, a nightdress for 10 years and one pair of shoes for one and a half years (see pp47-51 for more detail).[41]

There is also evidence from the *Family Expenditure Survey* which shows that living on incomes below the average means less money for food, for fuel to heat your home, and for clothing.

> I have not been able to go to the supermarket to get any weekly shopping for nearly twelve months now. We just live from day to day. About four days a week my food quota is a packet of biscuits a day.
>
> (Single parent of three, Merseyside)[42]

In 1987 a family with two children living on an income of under £175 a week (well above half the average income but the lowest measure of income provided by the *Family Expenditure Survey* for this type of family) spent:[43]

- £35.15 a week on food – £12.73 a week less than the average for families with two children
- £9.80 a week on clothing and footwear – £9.30 a week less than the average for families with two children
- £11.18 a week on fuel – £1.07 a week less than the average for families with two children
- £10.88 a week on household goods – £6.98 a week less than the average for families with two children.

> I haven't had any new clothes for four years.
>
> (Mother of one, S Wirral)[44]

The evidence is clear: in 1987, the levels of income (whether measured by supplementary benefit or 50% of average income) meant not being able to have access to the goods and resources which any affluent and civilised society ought to be able to provide.

Comparing the numbers

In 1987 both LIF and HBAI show that around 10 million people were living in poverty, whether measured by supplementary benefit or 50% of average income. However, the figures for earlier years are different:

- According to LIF , in 1979 around 6.1 people were living on or below supplementary benefit, 12% of the population; by 1987 there were 10.2 million – 19% of the population.
- According to HBAI, in 1979 around 4.9 million – 9% of the population – were living below 50% of average income, by 1987 this had doubled to 10.5 million – 19% of the population.

The reason for the difference in the statistics is obviously to do with what they measure. LIF looks at incomes in relation to supplementary benefit which generally rises in line with inflation, while HBAI looks at incomes in relation to the average. As we have seen, between 1979 and 1987 average income far outpaced the rise in inflation. Thus, the fact that the numbers living below 50% of the average income doubled between 1979 and 1987 (a rise that was steeper than the rise in the numbers measured by supplementary benefit) indicates the sharp rise in average incomes of which the poorest have had only the most meagre of shares. Both LIF and HBI bring considerable insights. Together they demonstrate what has happened to the numbers and incomes of people in the lower half of the income distribution. LIF has the advantage of enabling us to look at incomes in relation to a threshold set by Parliament and judge the effectiveness of the safety-net benefit; HBAI has the advantage of enabling us to look at poor people's incomes in relation to the rest of society.

What has happened since 1987?

The figures we have looked at stop in 1987. Since then unemployment has dropped, but is now on the rise again with talk of a recession in the air and our entry into the European Exchange Rate Mechanism. There have been further income tax cuts both for those on average incomes, but also especially for the rich. The most radical overhaul of social security was implemented in 1988. Some might argue that this makes the 1987 data irrelevant; after all perhaps the reforms have solved the problem of poverty. But on the government's own figures 43% stood to lose, 37% gain and 20% experienced no change in their incomes as a result of the changes. [45] All the evidence so far indicates that poverty is as entrenched as ever and some claimants have experienced real falls in their standard of living. For some people the experience of poverty may be more acute as they have to meet repayments for social fund loans and cover part of the cost of the poll tax and water rates from their basic benefit. None of these changes are contained in the figures above. But they suggest that in the future the picture may well be worse if unemployment continues to rise.

Conclusion

This chapter has discussed the problems of estimating poverty. This task is made much more difficult because no government of any political colour has established an official poverty line; there has been no attempt to relate rates of benefit to research into people's basic needs; government statistics which measure low income have been delayed, produced less frequently, have omitted earlier years for comparison, and have been changed, thus breaking continuity over time. [46] Lack of government information, research and sometimes deliberate obfuscation makes the choice of a poverty line particularly difficult.

Despite this, fact after fact shows that there are millions living in poverty. While the detail of statistics is technical, the issue of how and when they are published is crucial. It is only when the facts are exposed to the glare of publicity and open scrutiny that we can discuss the action and the policies which are so urgently needed.

Poverty has grown rapidly between 1979 and 1987. Whichever poverty line is used a fifth of our society was living in poverty in Britain in 1987. The poverty encountered by children is even greater than for society as a whole – around a quarter of children in Britain were living in poverty in 1987. Close to 3 million people were living below supplementary benefit – two-fifths of those because they have not claimed the benefit to which they were entitled. Above all, it is unemployment which is responsible for the rise in poverty. There have been important changes since 1979 with a decline in the proportion of pensioners in the poorest 10% of the population and a rise in the proportion of families with children and single people without children. While the average person has found that their real income has grown very comfortably, by 23% between 1979 and 1987, the poorest have seen a minuscule 0.1% rise in their real incomes (after paying for their housing costs). For the first time since 1949 the poorer half of society saw their share of overall income drop.

NOTES

1. DHSS, *Low Income Families 1985*, 1988.
2. P Johnson and S Webb, IFS Commentary c24, Poverty in Official Statistics: 2 reports, *Low Income Families 1979-1987*, 1990.
3. DSS, *Households below Average Income 1981-1987*, A statistical Analysis, Government Statistical Services, 1990.

4. Department of Employment, *Employment Gazettes* between 1979 and 1987.
5. *Economic Trends*, March 1980 and August 1990, HMSO 1980 and 1990, and *Low Paid Price Index*, from Low Pay Unit.
6. *see* note 4.
7. K Kiernan and M Wicks, *Family Change and future policy*, Family Policy Studies Centre and Joseph Rowntree Memorial Trust, 1990.
8. *see* note 2.
9. The Institute for Fiscal Studies was not able to reproduce the DSS figures exactly with the result that the figures are not entirely continuous.
10. *see* note 7.
11. *see* note 2.
12. S Mc Evaddy and C Oppenheim, *Christmas on the Breadline*, CPAG Ltd, 1987.
13. *see* note 2.
14. *see* note 2.
15. *see* note 2.
16. *see* note 3.
17. See DSS, *Households below Average Income*, page 71 for a discussion of the arguments for different measures of income, before and after housing costs.
18. *Economic Trends*, August 1990, HMSO 1990.
19. DSS, *Households below Average Income* (HBAI), tables F and annex 1 tables F, 1990.
20. DSS, *HBAI*, tables F2 and Annex 1 F2, 1990.
21. DSS, *HBAI*, tables F1 and annex 1 tables F1, 1990.
22. G Craig and C Glendinning, *The impact of social security change: The views of families using Barnardos pre-school services*, Barnardos, 1990.
23. *see* note 12.
24. DSS, *HBAI*, tables F3 and annex 1, table F3, 1990.
25. DSS, *HBAI*, table F3 and annex 1 F3, 1990.
26. DSS, *HBAI*, table C1 and F1 and annexes C1 and F1, 1990.
27. DSS, *HBAI*, Tables D1 and D2 and annex 1 D1 and D2, 1990.
28. DSS, *HBAI*, annex 1 table D1, 1990.
29. AB Atkinson, *DSS Report on Households below Average Income 1981-87*, paper for the Social Services Select Committee, 1990.
30. DSS, *HBAI*, table D2 and Annex 1 D2, 1990
31. *see* note 29.
32. DSS, *HBAI*, table H1 and annex 1 table H1, 1990.
33. DSS, *HBAI*, table G1 and annex 1 table G1, 1990.
34. *Dear Mr Moore*, CPAG Ltd for Save Child Benefit, 1987.
35. *see* note 33.
36. M Desai, 'Drawing the Line', in Peter Golding (ed) *Excluding the Poor*, CPAG Ltd 1986.
37. *Low Income Statistics*, Report of the Technical Review, Department of Health and Social Security, 1988. This shows in detail some of the problems of using supplementary benefit as a measure of poverty.
38. P Johnson and S Webb, *Counting people with Low Incomes*, Institute for Fiscal Studies, 1989.
39. This excludes the family premium which is paid per family receiving income support at a rate of £7.35 per week.
40. G Beltram, *Testing the Safety-Net*, Bedford Square Press, 1984.

41. J Bradshaw, *Budgeting on benefit*, Family Policy Studies Centre, 1987.
42. *see* note 12.
43. *Family Expenditure Survey 1987*, HMSO, 1988.
44. *see* note 12.
45. DHSS, *Impact of the Reformed Structure of Income Related Benefits*, 1987.
46. Specific examples of the difficulties with official statistics include the long delays in the publication of both the *Low Income Families* statistics and *Households below Average Income* – the 1987 statistics were published in the summer of 1990; until 1979 the *Low Income Families* statistics were published every year and from that time every two years (however it is now possible that the HBAI will be published each year in the future); a third example is the first set of HBAI, published in 1988, did not contain any figures for 1979, they have now been published in the appendix of the present edition in response to pressure from the Social Services Select Committee.

THREE

The consequences of poverty

Poverty curtails freedom of choice. The freedom to eat as you wish, to go where and when you like, to seek the leisure pursuits or political activities which others expect; all are denied to those without the resources . . . poverty is most comprehensively understood as a condition of partial citizenship.

Peter Golding, Excluding the Poor [1]

Poverty filters into every aspect of life. It is not simply about doing without *things*; it is also about being denied the expectation of decent health, education, shelter, a social life and a sense of self-esteem which the rest of society takes for granted.

In this chapter we look at some of the consequences of poverty: living on benefit, homelessness, debt and poor health.

Living on benefit

Going short

Some days, especially on a Wednesday, I have to decide whether to do without sugar and get a loaf, or do without a loaf and get two pounds of sugar . . . I always get the bread, I think (neighbours) will lend me a bit of sugar. You feel so small. (Joan, single mother) [2]

The evidence is very clear – living on benefit means going short. This section draws mainly on three reports – one which looks at the hardships faced by 140 families living on supplementary benefit in Tyne and Wear [3], and two reports by Barnardos, which describe people's views of life on income support [4]. The quotations come largely from the Barnardos' reports.

The 1989 Tyne and Wear study, *Living on the Edge*, found that

families on supplementary benefit:
- spent half as much as the average person on food;
- went without some items of clothing – 75% of men and women lacked two or more essential items of clothing, while 60% of their children were in the same situation:

The two littl 'uns could do with shoes, coats. They've got duffle coats but you can't put big duffle coats on when it's warm.

(Molly, mother of six)[5]

- cut down on heating – 54% did not use their central heating as much as they wanted; 27% used central heating only very occasionally; while a third never or rarely heated their bedrooms:

We've only got one electric fire in the lounge. The house is centrally heated but we got cut off two years ago due to arrears.

(Sarah and John with two children, living on income support)[6]

- had goods in bad condition – substantial minorities thought that their household goods were in poor condition; 28% thought this about their vacuum cleaners, 22% about their irons, 20% about their cookers, and 25% about their beds:

The cooker I've got is on its last legs. It was secondhand when I got it . . . I had an automatic washing machine given to me, but I can't afford to have it plumbed in.   (Vanessa, single mother)[7]

Isolation

Managing on benefit means little or no money for social activities. The Tyne and Wear study found that:
- families spent a great deal of time inside the house – children only spent 10% of their free time outside the home and women and men only 14% and 15% respectively. 75% of men and women had not been out for a meal in the last four weeks. Very few had gone to sports activities, cinema, or the theatre. Watching television and domestic activities were the main preoccupations inside the home:

It would be nice to go out but we can't afford it. I can't afford to go and see my family in East Anglia. They've only seen the baby once since she was born.

(Mary, single mother of two)[8]

In *Young and Jobless* by Susan McRae[9] young unemployed claimants describe how both a shortage of money and the isolation inherent in unemployment affect the chances of making friends:

Yes, it makes it harder . . . When you do go out, you can only stay out for so long, because you can't afford to buy so many drinks. Yes it is hard, it's more difficult than normal because they're all showing you what they've bought and that's depressing again . . .

(Adam, young unemployed man in Manchester)

I don't see a lot of people, so I feel I'm boring in conversation sometimes. I think back on what I've done and talk about that, but nothing concrete about what I've been doing over the last few months, because it's all the same. Days become the same, unless you break it up and do something.

(Katje, unemployed woman in Manchester)[10]

The impact on children

It hurts me when [my eldest daughter] asks for things and I can't afford them. If they go to a party they don't have a special dress or anything, which is horrible for them.   (June)[11]

The Tyne and Wear study found that families living on benefit were worried about the impact on their children.

TABLE 9	
Main restrictions on children	
Not enough space to play in	75%
Can't afford to get what they want	33%
No treats	20%
Few clothes	17%
No holidays/outings	16%
Nothing has changed for them	12%
Parents are irritable/bad tempered	2%
Feel different	1%

Depending on others

Struggling to make ends meet on benefit invariably means having to rely on friends and family. The Barnardos report shows that relatives are especially important at birthdays and Christmas.

Me mam was good because she bought them both a big present each. At Christmas, that's when me mam comes in, she really helps us out there.

(Andrea, single mother of two)[12]

But some people found that they resented the acute dependence brought about by shortage of money:

> I'd like a little bit of extra money so that if the kids do need a pair of trainers or a pair of shoes, I can go and get them without having to save up or hint at me mother to go halves with me. I would like to be more independent.
>
> (Carol, single mother of three) [13]

Battling with the benefit authorities

> The picture emerges from our survey of many concerned and diligent workers at the DHSS, both staff and management, trying, under great pressure and with diminishing resources, to service and sustain a system that has virtually collapsed. [14]

Living on benefit inevitably means doing battle with the Department of Social Security. The growth of unemployment and poverty has meant the extension of the means test to millions. Long waits in benefit offices to chase lost giros, to sort out mistakes, to be interviewed for a social fund review – these are the costs of being on the bottom rung of the social security ladder.

> I went down to the Housing Department and the lady there explained that the DHSS had failed to send authorisation. She was very sympathetic and sent the DHSS another memo and advised me to pay them another visit. I did although I had reached the stage of pregnancy where I could no longer wait for the requisite number of hours without recourse to a WC. I asked if I could use the toilet and was advised that it was not available to the public. It was suggested that I should look around for a public bar and use theirs. At almost eight months pregnant I had no intention of doing this, so was obliged to walk a quarter of a mile to the nearest public WC. I returned just in time to keep my place in the queue. [15]

Stress

Many people who have had to live on benefit for long periods talk of suffering from anxiety, strain and stress:

> I sit there and cry. Night after night some nights. Because I don't know what I'm going to do you know, for the kids' sake or my own.
>
> (Mrs Ward, unemployed) [16]

For some men there is great difficulty in coming to terms with the loss of the role as 'family provider':

I think it's just that you are on the existence level and that you are not supporting your family by your own endeavours. I think that demeans you more than anything else . . .   (Mr Ward, unemployed) [17]

In a survey of the living standards of 30 unemployed families, Jane Ritchie found that the wives of unemployed men were often under even greater stress than their husbands as many had to carry the burden of budgeting on very little money. [18] In the same survey, although some families thought that unemployment had brought them closer, a higher proportion thought that it had caused difficulties in their relationships. [19]

Living on benefit means cutting down on basics, it means no money for treats for the children, it means having to rely on friends and relatives to come to the rescue, it sometimes means being isolated and coping with a battered sense of self-esteem.

Homelessness

Homelessness is the most extreme aspect of poor housing conditions. Living in damp, draughty homes, waiting for repairs, being overcrowded, are all ways in which poverty directly impinges on people's lives.

London has a shanty town as large as might be expected in a Latin American city, but it is hidden. People live illegally in squats or in cramped, badly equipped hotels and crowded hostels. If they do not fall into a group that the government recognises as having a special need, or they cannot locate one of the very few spare spaces indoors, they find they have no choice but to survive on the streets. [20]

The *Households below Average Income* and the *Low Income Families* statistics cover only private households and therefore do not include people who are living in hostels, bed and breakfast hotels, or out on the streets. In other words, they exclude a large number of some of the most impoverished people in our society.

Numbers of homeless

Homelessness in Britain by Greve and Currie[21] catalogues the scale of homelessness today.

In 1989 the total number of homeless people was approximately 356,000 households or 686,000 people. This breaks down into:

- 140,000 households accepted as homeless by local authorities – an estimated 406,000 persons with 196,000 children. The great majority (80-85%) of these households were families with children. This is because of the stringent rules of the Homeless Person's Act which exclude single people from being a priority for housing. It is an increase of over four times the number in 1979 when 40,400 households were accepted as homeless; [22]
- 36,000 households in temporary accommodation, amounting to over 100,000 people;
- 180,000 single people who were homeless (in 1986).

In Inner London, the rate of homelessness is 4 per 1,000 compared with 1 per 1,000 in non-metropolitan areas. The National Federation of Housing Associations estimated that in 1989 the total number of single homeless people in London was between 121,000 and 125,000. [23]

Centrepoint in London conducted a survey of young people who came to stay at their night shelter. [24] They found that:

- 75% came from outside London to look for work;
- 41% had been living in care at some point in the past;
- over 78% had had to sleep rough;
- 77% were unemployed;
- serious problems with drug or alcohol abuse were rare, but one in three had been approached to become involved in prostitution;
- the people involved lived in extreme poverty – nearly half had no money at all; only 7% were not receiving income support, over half did not have enough money for food and over a third were begging.

The report concluded:

Restrictive social security and housing policies based on encouraging or forcing young people to 'stand on their own two feet or go home to mother' are for many of these young people based on a fallacy. They have no homes to which they can return. Their greatest wish is to stand on their own two feet but to do so they must have the possibility of finding work and a home.

Causes of homelessness

The principal reason for homelessness is a shortage of rented housing at reasonable prices. However, there are a number of immediate reasons for becoming homeless: breakdown of sharing arrangements, dissolution of a marriage or other partnership, loss of private rented tenancy, and other reasons such as mortgage default and rent arrears. [25] More recently, the changes in social security for young people have meant that they are now far more at risk of homelessness than in the past.

The risk of becoming homeless is higher for people living on low incomes, for people from ethnic minorities and for single parents:

- In 1988, a survey by the National Association of Citizens Advice Bureaux found that 53% of homeless clients were living on benefits and that in London 26% of homeless clients were black. [26]
- In 1987, 40% of households who were accepted as homeless by local authorities were single parents. [27]

The impact of homelessness

The security of a home is essential for health, a sense of well-being, and access to services and employment. *Prescription for Poor Health* documented the conditions for mothers and children living in bed-and-breakfast accommodation. [28] There are now 12,500 families living in bed-and-breakfast hotels in England and Wales. *Prescription for Poor Health* found:

- a high degree of stress among the women – 44% said they were unhappy most of the time, 41% were tired most of the time, 35% often lost their temper, 34% often couldn't sleep at night, 33% said the children got on top of them and 24% said they burst into tears for no reason:

  I'm turning into a cabbage here. Sometimes I think I'm going mad in this box of a room. [29]

- because of inadequate cooking facilities, over 33% of families never prepared a cooked meal for their families or did so less than once a week. In most cases, the women relied on take-aways and cafés. 25% of families had take-aways four times a week;
- babies born to mothers living in bed-and-breakfast accommodation were likely to have a lower birth weight than average;
- children were more likely to get infections and to suffer sickness;
- access to health care was very difficult.

A recent survey by Her Majesty's Inspectors found that many homeless children were not enrolled at school; others were frequently absent, performed poorly in class, and suffered from low self-esteem and expectations. [30]

The Bayswater Hotel Homelessness Project's recent report vividly describes the impact of living in bed-and-breakfast accommodation in contrast with having your own home.[31]

The women describe:

the cramped conditions

> In B&B there was no getting away from a bed. Everything was done on the bed – eating, sleeping, sitting and there was a baby two feet away. You felt under pressure. My nerves were terrible. Whereas when you're in your own place, baby's upstairs in her room. You've got a kitchen to cook in. You've got a table to sit and eat off. You've got a settee to sit on to watch the TV and a bed to go upstairs to sleep in. It's all completely different. You're more relaxed.
>
> (Carol)

the effect on children

> In your own flat you can cook, you are healthier, you're more hygienic. You try and keep everything clean in B&B, but it's really hard when you're all in one room. And the children, there's a hell of a lot of difference in the kids. It's taking a long time for my daughter to trust, because she thinks we're going to move.
>
> (Clare)

the effect on self-esteem

> I am treated differently now. You sometimes came across people who, when you said you were living in B&B, gave you that look. It's difficult to describe but you feel it. They make you feel small and nothing. Now that you have your own place you think, I can start living normally like other people. I can start sorting out my life. You start to think ahead.
>
> (Lisa)

Debt

> When I was four weeks overdue he came and sat outside the house for ages. Then he called to the door. When I tried to explain that I did not have the money he would not accept it. He told me to go to my sister's to get the money from her. Then, he sat in his car outside the house so none of us could go in or out from 8 in the evening until 12 midnight.
>
> (Mother of four, separated, £40 in arrears at the time)[32]

JOHN STURROCK/NETWORK

Living in damp, draughty homes, waiting for repairs, being overcrowded, are all ways in which poverty directly impinges on people's lives.

Indicators of debt

Debt is a major problem in the UK:

- In 1989, 131,276 income support claimants had automatic deductions from their basic benefit to pay for electricity at an average weekly amount of £9.08 and 134,004 for gas at an average rate of £8.67 per week. [33]
- In 1989, 51,235 income support claimants had automatic deductions to pay their rent arrears at an average of £2.03 per week. [34]
- In 1989, 352,048 income support claimants had automatic deductions to repay social fund loans at an average of £5.25 a week. [35]
- In May 1990, 2,434 income support claimants in Scotland had direct deductions from their basic benefit to pay poll tax arrears. [36]
- In 1989/90, 8,426 domestic customers were disconnected from their water supplies in England and Wales. [37] In 1984/85 the comparable figure was 2,149. [38]
- In 1988/89, there were 75,230 electricity disconnections, down from 98,894 in 1979/80. In 1989 there were 19,379 gas disconnections, a fall from 35,166 in 1979. [39]
- In 1988, building societies repossessed 16,150 homes in the UK, up from 2,530 in 1979. The latest figures show that in the first 6 months of 1990 14,390 homes were repossessed, that is nearly twice the figure of 7,390 for the second half of 1989 and more than the total for the whole of 1989. [40]

Who falls into debt?

Not surprisingly, many of the poorest households face acute debt problems. In *Credit and Debt in Britain*, Richard Berthoud and Elaine Kempson defined debts as difficulties in paying household expenses or consumer credit payments. [41] If a family said that they had a problem meeting an expense, this counted as a problem debt, and three or more of these counted as severe debt. The authors show how over a quarter of households with net weekly incomes of less than £100 had debts, compared with 15% for the average and 3% for households with incomes of above £400 a week (see Table 10):

> We're getting deeper and deeper into debt. I mean that hurts as well . . . One week he'll go and tell them that we can't pay, the next week I'll go. There was a time I'd hide if anybody knocked on the door. And if I went to the door, I'd stand there shaking. But now I just stand there and face them and tell them we haven't got the money.   (Mrs Ward) [42]

TABLE 10

Incidence of debt by income for non-pensioner households (%)

Net weekly income	Percentage with debts
Up to £100	28
£100-150	25
£150-200	15
£200-250	11
£250-300	11
£300-400	8
£400 or more	3
Average	15

SOURCE: Credit and Debt in Britain, R Berthoud and E Kempson, Policy Studies Institute, 1990

However, some families are more likely to be in debt than others – pensioners and people without children are less likely to be in debt. The more children a family has the greater the risk of debt. Single parents are particularly at risk:

- more than 4 out of 10 have one or more problem debts;
- 1 in 7 single parents are in severe debt. [43]

An earlier survey by Berthoud found that 74% of couples with children and 73% of single parents living on supplementary benefit had to borrow to make ends meet. [44]

The majority of debt problems are not linked to buying too many consumer durables; they are largely associated with housing, heating and essential services.

A survey of the living standards of people on supplementary benefit in Tyne and Wear [45] found that nearly all the families had debt problems, owing an average of £441 with a weekly repayment of £10.35 or 11.5% of weekly income. As the survey explains:

> For many families debts and their repayments created a vicious financial circle – debts, resulting from limited income themselves, created a financial burden which further limited their resources.

Poor health

Politicians who claim to care about disparities in health in our society are being disingenuous if they deny the association with poverty.

(British Medical Journal) [46]

Indicators of inequalities in health

Mortality statistics

While society as a whole has witnessed a significant decline in infant mortality, the gap between rich and poor remains substantial. *Mortality Statistics: perinatal and infant: social and biological factors* is published annually by the Office of Population Censuses and Surveys. [47] Table 11 shows the rates of perinatal and infant mortality by social class.

Perinatal mortality figures show that in 1987, 11 out of 1,000 babies born into Social Class V (unskilled workers) were still-born or died in the first week of birth; this compares to 7 out of 1,000 babies born into Social Class I (professional occupations). The figures for infant mortality (deaths occurring in the first year of life) show similar disparities – 12 out of 1,000 babies born into Social Class V died in their first year, compared

---

TABLE 11

Perinatal and infant mortality rates per 1,000 total births 1978-79 and 1987 compared by social class (legitimate births)

	Perinatal		Infant	
Social Class	1978-79	1987	1978-79	1987
I	11.9	6.8	9.8	6.9
II	12.3	7.0	10.1	6.7
III non-manual	13.9	7.8	11.1	7.1
III manual	15.1	8.1	12.4	7.7
IV	16.7	9.9	13.6	9.6
V	20.3	10.8	17.2	11.8
Others	20.4	9.9	23.3	12.4
Ratio of social class				
I-V	1.71	1.59	1.76	1.71

SOURCE: Mortality Statistics, Perinatal and Infant: social and biological factors, 1978-79 and 1987, Office of Population Censuses and Surveys, HMSO, 1990

to 7 out of 1,000 for Social Class I. (The differential between social classes is probably underestimated because it includes legitimate births only).

The gap between social classes has dropped very slightly for perinatal deaths between 1979 and 1987; for infant deaths it remains virtually the same.

An article in the *British Medical Journal* entitled 'The Black Report on Socioeconomic Inequalities in Health 10 years on' documents the increase in health inequalities. [48] For adults there is strong evidence to a show that class inequalities in health are widening. In 1971, the mortality ratio for Social Class V was 1.8 times that of Social Class I; by 1981 it had risen to 2.4 times. It is not only the gap between Social Classes I and V which has widened but also the gap between non-manual and manual workers.

Illness

> It's cold and damp. We've just got a fire in the children's room which took
> years to get. I've got bronchitis and so have the children.   (Julie) [49]

Poverty not only brings the risk of a shorter life-span, but it also means that the lives of adults and children are more likely to be ground down by illness and disability.

There are well established links between illness ('morbidity statistics') and social class. The *General Household Survey* examines these patterns, which it breaks down by sex and occupational grouping. [50] The Survey found that self-reported long-standing illness ranged from 27% of professional workers to 41% of unskilled manual workers. Other research reinforces this finding. A British heart study found that angina was twice as high amongst male manual workers than male non-manual workers in their middle age. The same study found that lung function was also worse in manual groups (this was partly independent of smoking patterns). Other studies have found that self-reported disability is twice as high in Social Class V as Social Class I. [51]

International studies confirm the link between class and mortality and morbidity rates. There is also evidence to show that health inequalities reflect income inequalities. The *British Medical Journal* article reports a comparative study of France, Sweden and England and Wales which found that England and Wales had greater health inequalities than Sweden but smaller than France. These patterns reflected the division of shares of income between rich and poor in those countries. [52]

Admission to hospital

A recent study of 593 children admitted to hospital in East London showed the link between material deprivation and going into hospital for
care.[53] It concluded that:

> . . . adverse socio-economic conditions have a deleterious effect on the health
> of children of all ages and result in their admission to hospital with various
> illnesses which may have been prevented had they lived in better circum-
> stances.

- The study also revealed that in 50% of cases neither parent of the
  child admitted was in employment (the average rate of unemployment for Hackney and Tower Hamlets was 23%);
- 59% of families were living in overcrowded conditions, of which
  30% were in severely overcrowded conditions (the average rate of
  overcrowding was 9% in Hackney and 10% in Tower Hamlets);
- 28% had inadequate water supply or sanitation;
- 24% reported significant damp;
- 28% said their heating was inadequate;
- 48% came from families whose head of household was Asian,
  African or Caribbean (these groups make up 18% of the population
  in Hackney and 11% in Tower Hamlets).

The authors concluded:

> Despite the rapid advances in medical technology in the twentieth century and
> the current economic growth of Britain, the majority of children admitted to
> an inner city hospital are suffering from infectious diseases such as respira-
> tory tract infections and gastroenteritis. Prevention of such conditions is more
> likely to be facilitated by improving housing conditions and poverty than by
> improving hospital and medical services.

The 1980 *Black Report* is perhaps the best known recent exposition of
the impact of poverty on poor health and premature death.[54] It was
updated in 1987 by *The Health Divide*[55] which showed the persistence of
health inequalities. Today the *British Medical Journal*[56] shows that this
gap is still widening and likely to become even more pronounced in the
future:

> The notion of the dispossessed and feckless 'underclass' that imposes costs on
> the rest of society and is to blame for most social ills is becoming popular.
> Such an idea has obvious consequences for social policy, yet it sits uneasily
> with the evidence from studies of differential mortality, which reiterate the
> fact that British society is stratified to a fine grain from top to bottom.

Conclusion

Poverty casts a wide net. It colours every aspect of life – meeting basic needs, joining in social activities, access to services, and the chance of good health. We have looked at just four different aspects of poverty – living on benefits, without a home of one's own, with debts and in poor health. Obviously, there are many other faces to the problem – poor housing, inadequate education, an environment that is dirty, noisy or dangerous, patchy transport facilities. Not all of these are experienced by all those in poverty or only by those in poverty; yet there is no doubt that people in poverty are much more likely to suffer each of these forms of deprivation, and often multiple deprivation, than people who are better off. Each of these topics deserves a book in its own right (and many have been written). However, the evidence presented here highlights the hardship and anguish experienced by people living in poverty. It shows how poverty means going short of the basics; it means not being able to turn the heating on, or replace household goods, and not being able to go out. Poverty carries with it the risk of debt and the risk of homelessness. Above all, poverty puts at risk that most precious thing: the chance of a healthy and long life.

NOTES

1. P Golding (ed), *Excluding the Poor*, CPAG Ltd, 1986.
2. Quoted in G Craig and C Glendenning, 'The impact of social security changes: the views of families living in disadvantaged areas', Barnardos Research and Development, 1990.
3. J Bradshaw and H Holmes, *Living on the edge: a study of the living standards of families on benefit in Tyne and Wear*, Tyneside CPAG, 1989.
4. *see* note 2, and G Craig and C Glendinning, 'The impact of social security changes: the views of families using Barnardos pre-school services', Barnardos, 1990.
5. *see* note 2.
6. *see* note 2.
7. *see* note 2.
8. Quoted in G Craig and C Glendinning, 'The impact of social security changes: the views of families using Barnardos pre-school services', Barnardos, 1990.
9. S McRae, *Young and Jobless*, Policy Studies Institute, 1987.
10. *see* note 9.
11. *see* note 8.
12. *see* note 8.
13. *see* note 2.
14. 'Out of Service', Greater London Citizens Advice Bureaux Service, 1986.
15. *Poverty 66*, CPAG Ltd, Spring 1987.

16. J Ritchie, *Thirty families: their living standards in unemployment*, DSS, 1990.
17. *see* note 16.
18. *see* note 16.
19. *see* note 16, and R Lampard, *An examination of the relationship between marital dissolution and unemployment*, The Social Change and Economic Life Initiative, ESRC, 1990.
20. D Canter et al, 'The faces of homelessness in London', Interim Report to the Salvation Army, January 1990.
21. J Greve with E Currie, *Homelessness in Britain*, Joseph Rowntree Memorial Trust, 1990.
22. *Social Trends 11, 1981* edition, Table 9.2, HMSO, 1980.
23. *see* note 21.
24. G Randall, *Homeless and hungry: a sign of the times*, Centrepoint, 1989.
25. *see* note 21.
26. 'Homelessness: a national survey of CAB clients', National Association of Citizens Advice Bureaux, 1988.
27. *see* note 7.
28. J Conway et al, *Prescription for poor health: the crisis for homeless families*, London Food Commission, Maternity Alliance, SHAC, Shelter, 1988.
29. *see* note 28.
30. *Independent*, 6 August 1990.
31. H Crane, *Speaking from Experience*, Bayswater Hotel Homelessness Project, 1990.
32. M Daly with J Walsh, 'Moneylending and low income families', Combat Poverty Agency, 1988.
33. *DSS Annual Statistical Enquiry 1989*, Income support, table 10.
34. *see* note 33.
35. *see* note 33.
36. *House of Commons Hansard*, 2 July 1990, col 460.
37. Office of Water Services as reported in the *Guardian*, 16 August 1990.
38. *House of Commons Hansard*, 30 October 1989, col 81, and 13 July 1987, col 343.
39. *Credit and Debt* (pp125-6), National Consumer Council, HMSO, 1990.
40. *House of Commons Hansard*, 5 February 1990, and Council of Mortgage Lenders as reported in the *Financial Times*, 15 August 1990.
41. R Berthoud and E Kempson, *Credit and Debt in Britain*, PSI, 1990.
42. J Ritchie, *Thirty families: their living standards in unemployment*, DSS, 1990.
43. R Berthoud, *Credit, Debt and Poverty*, Social Security Advisory Committee, Research Paper 1, HMSO, 1989.
44. *see* note 43.
45. *see* note 3.
46. Dr T Smith, *British Medical Journal*, Vol 301, 18-25 August 1990.
47. *Mortality statistics, perinatal and infant, social and biological factors*, 1978/79 and 1987, OPCS, HMSO, 1982 and 1990.
48. G Davy Smith, M Bartly, D Blane, 'The Black Report on socioeconomic inequalities in health: 10 years on', *British Medical Journal*, vol 301, 18-25 August 1990.
49. *see* note 2.
50. *General Household Survey 1987*, HMSO, 1989.
51. *see* note 48.
52. *see* note 48.
53. E P Carter et al, 'Material deprivation and its association with childhood hospital

admission in the East End of London', *Community Medicine*, Vol 15, No 6, June 1990.
54. P Townsend and N Davidson, *Inequalities in health: the Black Report*, Pelican, 1982.
55. M Whitehead, *The health divide*, Health Education Council, 1987.
56. *see* note 52.

FOUR

The causes of poverty

A factory closes its doors, casual workers are laid off, management is 'thinned out' – unemployment looms. A woman works a fifty-hour week doing two jobs to scrape together a living. A single mother struggles on benefit to meet the costs of her child – the only employment on offer would barely pay for her childcare. A man, prematurely retired because of chronic sickness, lives on invalidity pension which fails to cover the costs of his disability and his ordinary needs. *All these are causes of poverty*.

> The distribution of income and work need to be thought of together. To look only at incomes ignores the work done for it; to look only at work ignores the income received for it . . . Decisions about work are often not individual decisions but are affected by others, such as a partner and children. Opportunities and choices about income and work vary over the lifecycle.
>
> (David Piachaud) [1]

As Piachaud suggests, poverty is caused by not having access to decently paid employment. It is also the result of the extra costs of having a child or a disability or sickness which are met only by inadequate social security benefits. Poverty is particularly acute when these two factors combine. The risk of poverty is not shared out evenly – it depends on social class, on race and on gender. We look separately at race (Chapter 5) and women (Chapter 6). Below we explore some of the principal causes of poverty.

Unemployment

> I mean we can manage now – we haven't got a right lot of choice but to manage, have we? We're not rock bottom, but I think if it goes on much longer we could be going that way . . . It's getting harder to manage each

week . . . I'd love a holiday, really would love a complete break, but we haven't got much chance have we? I mean it's natural to want holidays and things isn't it? . . . I think everyone needs a holiday I don't care who you are. There's no way we can . . . but if you're working you don't have this problem.

(Mr Hawkins)[2]

Despite a decline in the number of people out of work since 1986, unemployment is still a major cause of poverty and it is on the rise yet again. In June 1990 the official rate of unemployment stood at 5.7% – 1,617,100 people in the UK. But, according to the Unemployment Unit, the government has changed the method of counting unemployed people 30 times since 1982, and in the process significantly reduced the number of people who appear to be unemployed.[3] The Unemployment Unit produces an alternative count of the unemployed which shows that unemployment stood at 8.5% in June 1990 – a total of 2,494,000.[4]

Unemployment was at its height in 1986. In June of that year there were 3,130,000 unemployed people, a rate of 11.2%. This was nearly three times the number in June 1979 when there were 1,069,000 unemployed people, a rate of 4%.[5] Long-term unemployment (people who have been unemployed for a year or more) is still a major problem. In July 1990, 32% of unemployed people were long-term unemployed, compared with 25% in July 1979. In 1987, there were 1,276,000 children living in families where the head had been out of work for a year or more.[6] Poverty is most intense amongst long-term unemployed families, because savings are used up, borrowing increases and household goods have to be replaced.

Benefits for unemployed people

A 17-year-old labourer in a bus depot in the North-East. He was expected to work 8-hour shifts 7 days a week. His wages for 56 hours were just £50. He was dismissed for trying to arrange to have one day off each week on alternate Saturdays and Sundays. Maximum disqualification was imposed but was reviewed eventually after representation from a citizens advice bureau.[7]

While unemployment soared benefits for unemployed people have been cut. Unemployed people can rely either on *unemployment benefit*, a national insurance contributory benefit, or on *income support* which is means-tested, or a combination of the two. The advantage of the former is that it is not means-tested and it is paid on an individual basis (so that an unemployed husband can receive unemployment benefit and his wife can continue to work without her earnings affecting his entitlement to benefit

for himself). However, because contributions have to be made and unemployment benefit lasts for just a year, many people have been forced
on to means-tested income support. In 1989/90 unemployment benefit
only supported 28% of unemployed people; the rest relied solely on
means-tested income support. [8] Some of the cuts and changes made to
benefits for unemployed people are listed here:

- In 1980, 5% was cut from unemployment benefit and only restored
  in 1983.
- In 1980, the earnings-related supplement to unemployment benefit
  was phased out, and finally abolished in 1982.
- In 1984, the children's additions for unemployment benefit were
  abolished.
- In recent years unemployment benefit has dropped as a proportion
  of average earnings: in 1971 for a single person it was 17.5% of
  average male earnings; this dropped to 16.2% in 1979 and then
  again to 12.9% in 1989. [9]
- The disqualification period from unemployment benefit when
  someone is 'voluntarily unemployed' has increased from 6 weeks
  to 6 months. During that time income support is *cut* by 20% or
  40%. [10]
- On the means-tested side, under the 1986 Social Security Act
  unemployed people receive no special premium to supplement
  their basic benefit – unlike other groups such as pensioners, people
  who are sick or who have a disability, families with children and
  single-parent families.
- The Social Security Act 1986 Act also brought in substantial cuts in
  benefit for young unemployed people. Young people aged 16 and
  17 can only receive income support if they have a Youth Training
  place or if they fall into one of the strictly defined categories of
  severe hardship. Otherwise they have to fend for themselves
  without support from the state. A lower rate of income support for
  18-24-year-olds was introduced. CPAG has estimated that between April 1987/88 and April 1990/91 income support for a
  single person living in his/her own home, aged between 18 and 24,
  has dropped by as much as 27% in real terms – £9.60 a week. [11]

Unemployment is not shared out evenly. Particular areas of the country
and certain sections of society bear the brunt (see Chapter 7 for more
detail). For example, in June 1990 unemployment ranged from 13.9% in
Northern Ireland to 3.7% in the South-East [12] (see Chapter 7).

As well as regional differences, the likelihood of unemployment is also determined by social class, race and sex (see Chapters 5 and 6 on race and women). For example, in 1989 the unemployment rate was 6 times as high for general labourers (14.9%) as for managerial and professional workers (2.4%). [13]

Families often experience multiple unemployment. According to one study, in 30% of all families where the 'head' was long-term unemployed, one or more other members of the family were also unemployed. [14]

Unemployment means *poverty*. One survey on living standards during unemployment showed that after three months of unemployment the average disposable income of families dropped to 59% of what it had been before unemployment. Families immediately reduced their spending on food, clothing and entertainments. Unemployment was also likely to cause psychological distress. 38% thought that the worst thing about being unemployed was being short of money, but 53% identified being bored, depressed, feeling dependent or losing control as being the prime cause of stress (see Chapter 3 for further detail). [15] If a man becomes unemployed there is a strong likelihood that his wife will give up paid work as well. This is because of the benefit rules – if the family is living on income support, a wife's earnings are offset against the benefit pound for pound (after a small amount of earnings is ignored). Thus, the woman would have to be able to command a high wage to make it worthwhile for the whole family to come off benefit. So unemployment in couples often means a sharp drop in income from a two-earner family to no earners at all. [16]

Poverty in employment

The pay is quite poor but it's better than unemployment benefit, even if it is only for a limited period . . . The problems I found with doing casual work is that you have no security, not knowing from one week to the next if your contract will be terminated . . . The insecurity of the casual job was the worst problem for me because of all my commitments at home.

(Liz, single mother of two) [17]

The poverty of low wages and poor working conditions is often still a hidden factor in the poverty debate. Government policies have specifically weakened employment rights. Rights against unfair dismissal were made conditional on longer length of service (two years for full-time workers). Many part-time workers fail to qualify at all. In 1982, the Fair Wages Resolution (which set minimum conditions of work for firms operating government contracts) was ended. In 1986, Wages Council protection for young workers was abolished, while, for adult workers, it was weakened. The proposal to abolish Wages Councils entirely has fortunately been put to one side, at least temporarily. However, the number of wages inspectors was cut substantially in 1986. The legislation to protect low-paid workers has been diluted and the means to enforce what remains of it weakened.

Alongside the deregulation of employment law new patterns of employment have changed the profile of the workforce. There has been a marked increase in both part-time and low-paid work coupled with a small increase in temporary work. Women are more likely to be in both part-time and temporary work. Many of these jobs are low paid with few employment and social security rights; a situation which not only creates poverty, but also stores it up for the future.

Between 1984 and 1989: [18]

- The number of full-time employees grew by 6%, while the number of part-time employees grew by 14%. In 1989, women made up 89% of the part-time workforce;
- The number of permanent workers grew by 10%, while the number of temporary workers grew by 12%. In 1989, women made up 58% of the temporary workforce.

In 1987, a survey of employers found that part-time and temporary workers were less likely to have fringe benefits than permanent workers: [19]

- 48% of temporary workers were entitled to sick pay and 22% to membership of a pension scheme.
- 78% of permanent part-time workers were entitled to sick pay and 32% to membership of a pension scheme.
- 94% of permanent full-time workers were entitled to sick pay and 78% to membership of a pension scheme.

High unemployment and the weakening of employment protection expose workers to low rates of pay. In 1989, 2 out of 5 full-time workers were living on low pay, defined as below two-thirds of median male earnings by the Low Pay Unit (£157 a week or £4.16 an hour). [20] The risk of low pay is much higher for black and other ethnic minority groups, and for women (see Chapters 5 and 6 respectively). Part-time workers are much more likely to be low-paid than full-time workers.

In 1989:

- 4.02 million part-time workers (78% of the part-time workforce) were low paid.

Children are more vulnerable to poverty than the rest of society. In 1987 3.1 million children, 1 in 4, were living in poverty.

- 4.85 million full-time workers (29% of the full-time adult workforce) were low paid.

This makes a staggering total of 8.88 million low-paid workers in Britain, or 41% of the adult workforce in 1989 – 71% of whom were women. These figures demonstrate a deterioration in the situation since 1979 when 36% of the adult workforce were low paid.

Many low-paid workers, although often on means-tested benefits, still pay tax. This means that a growing number of people are caught in the *poverty trap* (where a large part of any rise in earnings is withdrawn through increased tax and reduced social security benefits). For example, in 1985/86, 290,000 families stood to lose between 70 pence and 99 pence out of every extra £1 they earned.[21] Although the most extreme form of the poverty trap (whereby someone could lose more than a pound for each extra pound of earnings) has been eliminated, the poverty trap now catches more people. By 1990/91 the figure had risen to 410,000.[22]

Having children

I struggle to hold down a full-time job, which is both physically and mentally tiring, and add to this the extra work involved in packing lunches, trying vainly to cook nourishing meals in the evening and daily trying to save money by cutting corners.   (Single mother of two)[23]

Poverty ebbs and flows through the lifecycle, but one particularly vulnerable period is when children are born into the family. Children bring extra costs for essentials and they usually mean that the mother stops work for a while. It is this combination of higher costs and lower income which pushes families – and particularly single mothers – into poverty. The evidence is stark. The income of the poorest quarter of the population *with* children is substantially lower than the income of those *without* children:[24]

- Using disposable income adjusted for family size, in 1988 the *Family Expenditure Survey* revealed that the bottom quarter of couples with no children had incomes of £173 a week on average. This fell to £138 for a couple with 2 children and £82 for a couple with 4 children in the bottom quarter.
- For single parents the effects were even worse. In 1988, the average income of the bottom quarter of single people without children was £120 a week. This was almost halved to £66 for a

single parent with one child in the bottom quarter (ie, only 50% of the figure for those without children).

Alongside the *direct costs* of providing for children's needs in terms of food and clothing etc, there are also the *opportunity costs* incurred by one parent's (usually the mother's) time out of work and her reduced earnings on return to work. On top of this are the *hidden costs* of unpaid caring tasks (see Chapter 6). [25]

In 1990:

- It was estimated that the cost of a healthy diet for a pregnant woman was £17.72 a week. This is hard to attain if you are on benefit, since such a diet is 48% of income support for a single person aged over 25, and 31% for a couple aged over 25. [26]
- Using Mothercare's catalogue, CPAG found that the cost of maternity clothes and the outlay on a baby can be as much as £1,050. [27]
- Using the National Foster Care Association's recommended allowances for foster parents, CPAG estimated that the average direct cost of bringing up a child to the age of 16 can be as much as £42,000. [28]

Benefits for families with children

While the government claims to have recognised the particular needs of many families and children, in practice, support for most families with children has been declining:

- In 1990, *child benefit* was frozen for the third time at £7.25 – a loss of £1.35 per child per week in total. Unbelievably, the real value of child support (that is, child benefit now, compared with the old family allowances and child tax allowances) for a standard rate tax-paying family, is worth much less now in real terms than 30 years ago[29]:

    The £7.25 a week does not go anywhere near paying for things they need. Recently two pairs of shoes cost me £31 for my two children and I get £14.50 a week. It doesn't even pay for one pair . . . It should be increased, not lessened.   (Mrs D, mother of two)[30]

- *Family credit* was introduced as part of the 1986 Social Security Act to help families with children in low-paid work. Although it is more generous than its predecessor (family income supplement), and goes to more people, there are still major drawbacks:

- in 1988/89 only half of those families entitled to family credit claimed it; [31]
- the gains have been offset for some people by substantial cuts in housing benefit for people in paid work.
- There is considerable evidence to show that the income support personal allowances for children still don't meet the *minimum* costs of a child. In 1990, CPAG calculated that income support for children provided only 83% of the *minimum costs* of a 5-year-old and 68% of those of an 8-year-old. [32]
- Although families with children now get premiums under income support, many have lost out as a result of the social security changes implemented in 1988. CPAG has estimated that between April 1987/88 and April 1990/91 a couple with 2 children getting income support have lost 4% in real terms or £3.60 (this assumes they received a single payment and a heating addition). Over the same period a lone parent has lost 2% in real terms or 95 pence (assuming no single payment was received). [33]
- The introduction of the social fund has hit families with children particularly badly, primarily because they were more likely to receive single payments (grants) under the old system. The budget for the social fund has barely risen since its introduction and families with children find it very difficult to get community care grants and instead they must rely on loans. Rather than helping with problems, loans simply compound them:

> Before they would give you money for things you desperately needed. Now you have to get a loan and I can't afford to pay it back . . . I don't agree with the loans, the problem is paying them back and you don't get enough.   (Denise, single mother of three) [34]

Disability and sickness

To be disabled, therefore, is also to be disadvantaged. It means regularly being unable to participate in the social and economic activities which most people take for granted. It means confronting the negative attitudes of others and sometimes internalising those reactions until they become part of the psychological accoutrements of disability itself. However, at the same time it can also mean gaining the additional insight that comes from encountering a wider range of experiences. It can mean overcoming enormous challenges, leading to a sense of achievement and fulfilment.

(Women and Disability) [35]

Disability brings with it poor employment opportunities, lower earnings, high dependency on benefit and greater costs. Together this means people with disabilities have to live on very low incomes often with little chance of being able to participate fully in society.

The latest survey of disability in Britain was carried out by the Office of Population Censuses and Surveys (OPCS) between 1985 and 1988 and constituted the most complete picture of disability in Britain today. [36] According to the survey, there are 6.2 million adults (14% of all adults) and 360,000 children (3% of all children) with one or more disability. The Disability Alliance believes that even this large figure is an underestimate. [37] Most people with disabilities live in the community – only 7% of adults with a disability (400,000) and under 2% of children (5,500) with a disability live in a communal establishment. The following statistics portray the stark poverty of people with disabilities in comparison with the rest of the population. [38] In 1985:

- 34% of non-pensioner adults with a disability were living in poverty below 50% of average income, in comparison with 23% of the general population. Only 19% had incomes above the average, in comparison with 42% of the general population. (These figures are not the same as in *Households below Average Income* as different assumptions are used.)
- The average income for non-pensioners with a disability was 72% of the incomes for non-pensioners in general (that is, less than three-quarters). This is because they are much less likely to have earnings.
- The incomes of pensioners with a disability were similar to those without a disability because so many pensioners live on low incomes.

It is not only having less money coming in which puts people with a disability at risk of poverty, but also the extra money they have to spend to cope with their disability. The report estimated that in 1985:

- 16% of adults with a disability had made a lump-sum purchase for special equipment or furniture related to their disability, averaging £78 over the past year.
- On average, adults with a disability were spending an extra £6.10 a week on regular extra costs such as prescriptions, home services, fuel, clothing, and bedding. This extra spending varied with the

severity of the disability – £3.20 for people with the least severe disability, rising to £11.10 for people with the most severe disability. On average 8% of income was spent on disability-related expenses.

Benefits for people with disabilities

Poor employment chances often mean lifelong dependence on inadequate and patchy social security benefits. In 1985, the OPCS survey found that over half (58%) of the income of adults with a disability came from state benefits in comparison with 13% for the general population.[39] However, the government has made some small improvements in benefits for people with disabilities but recent years have nevertheless seen significant cuts:

- Many people with disabilities lost out substantially as a result of the 1988 social security changes. This is because under the supplementary benefit system many people with both mild and severe disabilities received extra weekly payments to help with special diets, extra baths, extra laundry and so on. These additions were replaced by disability and severe disability premiums. Some people with a mild disability – eg, a child with chronic asthma – find they are not entitled to a premium at all. For others, whose extra needs are considerable, the premiums are not sufficient to meet the demands. CPAG has estimated that between April 1987/88 and April 1990/91, income support for a single person with a disability premium represents a drop in real terms of 15% (or £8.75 a week) in comparison with supplementary benefit (for a claimant who used to get four extra weekly payments under supplementary benefit).[40]
- Like other benefits, invalidity pension has not kept pace with earnings. In 1971 invalidity pension was 17.5% of average earnings for all men, in 1979 it had risen to 20.4%, but by 1989 it had fallen to 16.3%.[41]
- The new disability benefits proposed (some already in place) as part of the government's response to the OPCS surveys, only touch the surface of the problem. They help some 850,000 people out of the 6.5 million identified as having disabilities in the surveys. While they bring increases in some areas, they bring cuts in others.[42]

Sickness and disability affect, in turn, how much relatives who take on caring responsibilities can earn, and often ensure that both carers and people with disabilities are pushed further into poverty. In 1985, one-fifth (20%) of adults aged 45 to 64 were looking after someone who was sick, elderly or had a disability. Women were more likely to be carers than men – nearly a quarter (24%) of women aged 45 to 64 were carers, compared with 16% of men. [43]

Piece by piece, the OPCS surveys build up a picture of the disadvantage and poverty encountered by people with disabilities. Adults and children with disabilities are frequently locked out of society by a combination of low earnings, poor jobs, low benefits and services which barely scratch the surface of need.

Old age

The inequalities in working life between employment and unemployment, low-paid and high-paid work, between men and women, are compounded in old age. There are still two nations of the elderly: elderly people who are dependent on income support (the replacement for supplementary pension), and in council or private rented housing without private or occupational pensions and with few or no savings; and elderly people who have the generous bonuses from a lifetime's secure and well-paid employment. [44]

In 1988, elderly people (over pension age) numbered 10.4 million in Great Britain, or 18% of the population. [45] Because of high unemployment, elderly people are far less likely to be economically active today than they were twenty years ago. In 1988, pensioners were dependent on social security benefits for an average of 44% of their household income (the remainder coming from savings, occupational pensions and small earnings), in contrast to 11% for the average non-elderly household. [46]

Women make up around two-thirds of the elderly population. They are far more likely than men to be poor pensioners because of their lower earnings, interrupted work patterns and greater life expectancy. In 1988 there were nearly three times as many women pensioners as men dependent on income support. [47]

Benefits for pensioners

Although elderly people have a very high risk of falling into poverty (see Chapter 2), the government has weakened financial protection for some of the poorest pensioners:

- The decision in 1980 to uprate the retirement pension by rises in prices alone (until that date retirement pension was uprated by earnings or prices, whichever was higher) has meant substantial losses for pensioners. The retirement pension would be £11.75 higher for a single person and £18.95 higher for a couple had it been uprated by this method since then. [48]

- Not surprisingly, the retirement pension has dropped as a proportion of earnings since 1980: the retirement pension for a single person was 17.5% of male average earnings in 1971; 20.4% in 1979 and 16.3% in 1989. [49]

- The new disability benefits proposals do nothing to help the 4.2 million pensioners with disabilities.

- The Social Security Act 1986 has both weakened the State Earnings Related Pension Scheme (SERPS) and increased incentives to take out a private pension. In years to come, this will increase poverty for many elderly people. Private pensions mirror inequalities in the labour market, leaving those who have been unemployed, or low paid, or who have worked part time, in poverty in their old age, while providing large incomes for those who have had permanent and well-paid jobs.

- Many pensioners on income support have experienced a drop in their living standards. CPAG has estimated that, between April 1987/88 and April 1990/91, a pensioner couple getting income support have lost 8% in real terms – that is £6.50 a week – (this assumes that they received a weekly payment for diabetes and heating). [50]

Conclusion

Poverty is largely determined by two factors – access to the labour market and extra costs. Access to the labour market depends on a number of different factors – amongst them, class, race, and sex. We have seen how the rise in unemployment has pushed millions into poverty. Getting a job is not necessarily the answer to poverty if that job pays paltry earnings, has long hours and poor working conditions – the poverty of unemployment is simply translated into the poverty of work. Extra costs often come with changes in the lifecycle. For example, the extra costs of having a child combined with being out of the labour market bring poverty to families with children and in particular to single mothers. Disability and sickness also bring extra costs, but at the same time less or no opportunity to be in paid work. And finally, old age carries such a high risk of poverty because it is a time of life when there are few earnings and as old age progresses no earnings at all. In each of these cases social security benefits have failed to pull people out of poverty, often leaving them to manage on the most meagre of incomes.

Coming to grips with the causes of poverty involves a commitment to a wide-ranging strategy. CPAG believes that some of the following policies would begin to set the agenda:

• An economic strategy which has the reduction of unemployment at its heart.

• A strong commitment to training and re-training.

• A statutory minimum wage for full- and part-time workers, equal pay for men and women, pro-rata employment rights for part-time workers.

• A large increase in child benefit and a substantial increase in the availability of subsidised childcare.

• A comprehensive disability income which both meets the cost of disability and provides an income for people with disabilities who cannot work or whose ability to work is affected by their disability.

• Steps towards a non-means-tested social security system without contribution conditions; individual entitlement to benefits and benefits paid at an adequate level.

NOTES

1. D Piachaud, 'The distribution of income and work', *Oxford Review of Economic Policy*, Vol 3, No 3, 1988.
2. Quoted in J Ritchie, *Thirty families: their living standards in unemployment*, DSS, 1990.
3. 'Creative Counting', Unemployment Unit, 1990.
4. 'Working Brief', August/September, Unemployment Unit, 1990.
5. *Employment Gazette*, Historical Supplement No 1, Unemployment Statistics, Department of Employment, April 1989.
6. K Kiernan and M Wicks, *Family changes and future policy*, Family Policy Studies Centre and Joseph Rowntree Memorial Trust, 1990.
7. Quoted in D Byrne & J Jacobs, *Disqualified from benefit*, Low Pay Unit, 1988.
8. *The Government's Expenditure Plans 1990/91 to 1992/93*, Cmnd 1014, HMSO, 1990.
9. *Abstract of statistics for index of retail prices: social security benefit and contributions*, Table 5, DSS, August 1989.
10. *see* note 7.
11. C Oppenheim, 'Holes in the safety net', CPAG Ltd, 1990. These calculations do not take into account transitional protection which provided cash protection for many claimants. They simply compare income support in 1990/91 with supplementary benefit in 1987/88.
12. *see* note 2.
13. *Employment Gazette*, 'Characteristics of the unemployed', Department of Employment, May 1990.

14. C Hakim, 'The Social Consequences of Unemployment', *Journal of Social Policy*, Vol 11, part 4, 1982.
15. P Heady and M Smyth, *Living standards during unemployment*, Vol 1: The Results, HMSO, 1990.
16. For more detail, see J C Brown, *Why don't they go to work?: Mothers on benefit*, Social Security Advisory Committee, HMSO, 1989.
17. Quoted in T Potter, *A temporary phenomenon*, West Midlands Low Pay Unit, 1989.
18. *Employment Gazette*, Department of Employment, April 1990.
19. D Wood and S Smith, *Employers' Labour Use Strategy*, Research Paper 63, Department of Employment.
20. *Low Pay in Great Britain and the Regions*, Low Pay Unit, Parliamentary Briefing No 1, 1990.
21. The New Review, No. 3, Low Pay Unit Parliamentary briefing, April/May 1990.
22. *House of Commons Hansard*, col 790, 5 April 1990.
23. Quoted in S McEvaddy, 'One good meal a day', CPAG Ltd, 1988.
24. D Piachaud, 'Poverty and Social Security', unpublished paper for the Select Committee on Social Services, 1990.
25. C Oppenheim, 'The Cost of a Child', CPAG Ltd, 1990.
26. Based on calculation from Maternity Alliance; *see* note 25.
27. *see* note 25.
28. *see* note 25.
29. *House of Commons Hansard*, 6 November 1989, cols 459-60.
30. Quoted in 'Dear Mr Moore', CPAG Ltd, 1988.
31. *House of Commons Hansard*, 27 November 1989, col 144.
32. *see* note 25.
33. *see* note 7.
34. Quoted in G Craig and C Glendinning, *The impact of social security changes: the views of families using Barnardos pre-school services*, Barnardos Research and Development, 1990.
35. S Lonsdale, *Women and disability*, Macmillan, 1990.
36. *Office of Population Censuses and Surveys, Surveys of disability in Great Britain*, Reports 1-6, HMSO, 1988/89.
37. Disability Alliance, 'Briefing on the "First Report" from the OPCS surveys of disability', 1988.
38. *see* note 36. Report 2, 'The financial circumstances of disabled adults living in private households'.
39. *Family Expenditure Survey 1985*, HMSO, 1986. We have used an earlier date for comparative purposes with the disability survey which took place in 1985.
40. *see* note 11.
41. DSS, *see* note 9.
42. Linda Lennard, *Welfare Rights Bulletin 97*, CPAG Ltd, August 1990.
43. H Green, 'Informal Carers', *General Household Survey*, HMSO, 1988.
44. P Townsend, *Poverty in the UK*, Penguin, 1979.
45. *Population Studies*, HMSO, 1990.
46. *Family Expenditure Survey 1988*, Table 22, HMSO, 1990.
47. *Social Security Statistics 1989*, DSS, HMSO, 1989.
48. *House of Commons Hansard*, col 607, 4 July 1990.
49. DSS, *see* note 6.
50. *see* note 7.

FIVE

Race and poverty

Blackness and poverty are more correlated than they were some years ago. In spite of government concern with racial disadvantage, and the undoubted limited success of positive action and equal opportunities in helping to create a black middle class, the condition of the black poor is deteriorating.

K Amin and K Leech [1]

Despite often shocking levels of poverty faced by black people and other members of ethnic minorities, there is still precious little social policy research about race and poverty. *Households below Average Income* – the source of official data about low-income families – contains no breakdown of statistics by ethnic origin. Neither did the *Low Income Families* statistics. [2] The principal sources of information on racial inequality are the *Labour Force Survey by Ethnic Origin* [3], the Policy Studies Institute survey of 1982 (now becoming out of date) and many useful local surveys. [4]

Below we look at some of the indicators and causes of poverty broken down by ethnic origin. [5]

Indicators of Poverty

Unemployment [6]

- Unemployment rates for black and other ethnic minority groups have always been much higher than for white people. Although the gap has narrowed since 1984, it remains substantial. In the period 1986-88 the male unemployment rate for black people and other ethnic minority groups was 17 per cent, compared with 10 per cent for white people. The unemployment rates for black women and women in other ethnic minority groups were almost double those of white women: 16 per cent compared to 9 per cent (see Table 12).

• For young people the disparity in unemployment rates is even greater. In the period 1986-88 28 per cent of Caribbean, 22 per cent of Indian and 31 per cent of Pakistani or Bangladeshi young people aged between 16 and 24 were unemployed, compared to 15 per cent of white people.

• Even with qualifications black people and members of other ethnic minorities are still more likely to experience unemployment due to discrimination. In the period 1986-88 the unemployment rate was 7% for black people and other ethnic minorities with higher qualifications, and only 4% for white people with the same qualifications. For black people and other ethnic minorities with 'other qualifications' the unemployment rate was 17% compared to 9% for white people who were similarly qualified.

> If you can't be looked at and be seen as white, then you're going to be disadvantaged in employment. It's as simple and as easy as that.
>
> (Winston, young black unemployed adult) [7]

TABLE 12

Unemployment rates by sex, age and ethnic origin; average: spring 1986 to 1988, Great Britain (%)

	Men		Women	
	All aged 16 and over	16 to 24	All aged 16 and over	16 to 24
White	10	16	9	14
Ethnic Minority Groups:				
All	17	26	16	24
Caribbean/Guyanese	22	31	15	25
Indian	12	*	16	*
Pakistani/Bangladeshi	27	*	*	*
All other origins	14	*	14	*

* Sample too small

SOURCE: Employment Gazette, Department of Employment, March 1990

Low pay

I work 40 hours a week in the factory and my take-home pay is between £55 and £66 per week. Last year I started a homeworking job which I can do most evenings and weekends. For this I get paid £15-£20 per week depending on the number of overalls I manage to complete. This money adds towards the household budget and occasionally for clothes for the children . . . With the domestic duties and two jobs I have very little time to relax. I don't even have time to fall ill or complain about a backache. I know the work has to be done, as the man would soon come to collect the overalls. My only social life is going to local weddings.   (Mrs P, 42 years old, Asian, with three children) [8]

A sizeable proportion of people living in poverty work in low-paid jobs. Black people and other ethnic minority groups are more likely to work for low wages than their white counterparts.

The *New Earnings Survey* – the principal source for statistics on earnings – does not provide a breakdown of earnings by ethnic origin. However, it is clear that black people are clustered in industries which have particularly low wages. In 1988, 53% of men from ethnic minorities worked in the distribution, hotels and catering sectors, compared to 36% of white men. [9] Wages in this sector are particularly low. For example in hotels and catering 52% of men earned less than £130 a week in 1988. Although white men work in some very low-paying sectors, such as agriculture, only 3% of the total white workforce are agricultural workers. As a whole, 55% of men from ethnic minorities worked in industries where 30% or more of the workforce earned below £130 per week, compared to 33% of white men. [10]

Figures from the Policy Studies Institute (PSI) show that in 1982 Caribbean and Asian men earned less than white men (see Table 13). [11] White women earn more than Asian women, but less than Caribbean women. Part of the explanation for this is that Caribbean women are more likely to work full time, to undertake more shift work and be based in large unionised public sector work places, where wages are somewhat higher. In addition, women as a whole are concentrated in the low-paid sector of the economy, so there is less room for disparities based on race.

As well as suffering low pay, a large percentage of black people find themselves experiencing some of the worst working conditions. PSI research showed that differences in working conditions also follow the lines of race. On the whole, black men and women were far more likely to work shifts, alternating shifts and nights [12]:

TABLE 13
Gross earnings of full-time employees, 1982

	Median Weekly earnings	
	Men	Women
White	£129.00	£77.50
Caribbean	£109.20	£81.20
Asian	£110.70	£73.00

SOURCE: Black and White Britain, C Brown, Third PSI Survey, Gower, 1984

- 33% of Asian and 29% of Caribbean men worked regular shifts compared to 20% of white men.
- 14% of Asian and 18% of Caribbean women worked regular shifts, compared to 11% of white women.
- 7% of Asian men and 4% of Caribbean men and women worked nights only, compared to 1% of white men and 1% of white women.

I've worked nights on the wards for years and it really does put a strain on you, there's no question about it. You get a lot of nurses and auxiliaries who suffer from the stress-related illness – hypertension, heart trouble, kidney problems, high blood pressure – you name it, they all come from those broken sleep patterns from the night shift. You can't just go home and go to sleep during the day if you've got kids. When you come in from work, you've got to get them ready for school, do the shopping, do the housework, do the washing, and by the time you've finished it's three o'clock and time to collect them from school again, so you just don't get any rest . . . What happens is you just adjust in time to getting less sleep than everyone else, but over the years that takes its toll.   (The Heart of the Race) [13]

Benefits

There are no government statistics which give a breakdown of benefit claimants by ethnic origin. However, the PSI report shows that black people are more likely to receive certain benefits (see Table 14) with the exception of retirement pension (see p88). [14] It is difficult to interpret these statistics as there is also some evidence to show that black people are less likely to claim benefits, so these figures are likely to *under-estimate* the true picture of low income.

A higher proportion of Caribbean and Asian people claimed unemployment benefit and family income supplement. Caribbean people were also more likely to be dependent on supplementary benefit/pension than white people. (The low figure for Asian people may be due to the underclaiming of benefits – see p89.)

TABLE 14			
All households	**White**	**Caribbean**	**Asian**
Per cent in receipt of . . .			
Child Benefit	34	60	75
Unemployment Benefit	7	17	16
Family Income Supplement	1	5	2
Supplementary Benefit/Pension	14	20	11
Retirement/Widow's Pension	35	6	6

SOURCE: Black and White Britain, C Brown, Third PSI Survey, Gower, 1984

Causes of poverty

The persistence of high levels of poverty for black people and minority groups is due to a number of different factors:

* Immigration policy has curtailed access to welfare services forcing some people from abroad to rely on family support.
* Inequalities in the labour market are founded on deeply embedded discriminatory employment practices. This has left black people highly exposed to the economic restructuring which has taken place through the seventies and eighties.
* Family patterns and the age structure of ethnic minority groups mean that some groups are more likely to be vulnerable to poverty.
* Social security policies have been directly and indirectly discriminatory, often leaving black people without support from the state.
* The racism and discrimination in society as a whole have often excluded black people from employment opportunities and access to welfare.

Immigration policy and poverty

Black people's experience of poverty has been fundamentally shaped by immigration policy. [15] Legislation has been geared to placing immigrants in particular jobs – for black people this has meant low-paid work in poor conditions. Immigration policy has also curbed access to welfare services. After the 1971 Immigration Act, the wives and children of Commonwealth citizens could only enter the United Kingdom if a sponsor could support and accommodate them without recourse to 'public funds'. 'Public funds' – clearly defined for the first time in 1985 – consisted of supplementary benefit (now income support), housing benefit, family income supplement (now family credit) and housing under Part III of the Housing Act 1985 (Housing the Homeless). The effect of these policies has often been to cause great financial hardship, as people struggle to survive without help from the state. These policies have also meant that some families have been forced to live apart in different parts of the world because UK citizens cannot afford to support dependants without some support from the state. More fundamentally, the legislation has reinforced a climate of opinion where black people are seen as 'outsiders', unwelcome in British society.

Inequality in the labour market

Immigrant workers were sucked into the economy where they were needed, whatever their qualifications – into those jobs that white people were becoming less inclined to do. The availability of jobs during labour shortages therefore laid the basis for the occupational inequalities that have persisted since.

(*Race Relations and Discrimination*) [16]

The poverty of black people is rooted in old inequalities in the labour market. Black people still work in the manufacturing and manual work for which they were recruited in the fifties and sixties.

In the period 1986-88, 28% of Caribbean and Guyanese men, and 36% of Pakistani and Bangladeshi men, held non-manual positions, compared to 47% of white men. Indian men were the exception – 54% held managerial posts. On the other hand, 72% of Caribbean and Guyanese men and 64% of Pakistani and Bangladeshi men were in manual occupations compared to 53% of white men. For women the hierarchical differentiation is not as marked (although the figures exclude women from Pakistan and Bangladesh and are therefore partial). Caribbean and Guyanese women were slightly more likely to work in manual occupations than white women. [17]

The segregation of black workers into certain industries and into manual work has particularly exposed them to both the decline of manufacturing industry and the rise in unemployment. Unemployment is a much higher risk for people in manual work (see p67).

Around 70 per cent of Asians and 81 per cent of Caribbeans live in Metropolitan County areas, largely in inner cities, compared to 31% of white people. [18] Living in inner city areas has meant that black people have faced the brunt of the exodus of industry from city heartlands. The consequence has been high unemployment for black people.

Broad economic changes are compounded by discrimination. A report on employment in Rochdale found that working in the textile industry increased the chances of becoming unemployed and that this probability increased significantly for Asian people. [19] A quarter of Asian people interviewed thought that being Asian had affected their employment opportunities. The report identifies the causes of unemployment for Asian workers:

> . . . Many firms have closed down their night shifts where traditionally most Asians have worked. Secondly, there has been a major reduction of routine, non-skilled manual work where Asians were traditionally concentrated. Thirdly, many Asians lacked sufficient seniority to have avoided being made redundant in this period. Finally, fewer new textile jobs are advertised formally and recruitment tends to be based upon . . . recommendations from relations and friends. [20]

The evidence of racial inequality in new forms of employment is still tentative. However, what there is suggests that new jobs in insurance, banking and finance have tended to reinforce racial inequalities in the labour force. For example, a report on the Asian community's access to employment opportunities generated by computer-related technology in the London Borough of Ealing found that Asians were under-represented in the higher echelons of information technology industry. [21] A similar report examining the barriers facing Caribbeans in the computing industry in the London boroughs of Hammersmith and Fulham concluded:

> Discrimination and stereotyped views held by many people about black people put them at a disadvantaged position when they come to look for jobs in information technology. [22]

Family patterns

The age profile of black people is younger than white people. In the period 1985-87: [23]

- 25% of Caribbean or Guyanese, 31% of Indian, 43% of Pakistani, 50% of Bangladeshi and 20% of white people were aged under 15.
- 33% of Caribbean or Guyanese, 27% of Indian , 25% of Pakistani, 21% of Bangladeshi and 22% of white people were aged between 16 and 29.
- 7% of Caribbean or Guyanese, 5% of Indian, 2% of Pakistani, 1% of Bangladeshi and 21% of white people were aged 60 and above.

The younger age profile means that black people and other ethnic minorities are disproportionately affected by government policies such as freezing child benefit and cuts in income support for young people. On the other hand, there are fewer black people and other ethnic minorities among pensioners. This means that as a whole they are less affected by the poverty which pensioners experience. However, although small in number, black pensioners are in fact more likely than white pensioners to be living on lower incomes because of social security rules which are indirectly discriminatory. As the black and ethnic minority population grows older, they will become more vulnerable to the poverty which afflicts pensioners.

Family patterns also vary considerably between different ethnic groups. Single parenthood is lower amongst Asian people than white people, but higher amongst Caribbean people:[24]

- 4.8% of Asian families were single parent families;
- 43.4% of Caribbean families were single parent families;
- 17.6% of other ethnic minority families were single parent families;
- 11.8% of white families were single parent families.

As we have seen, the risks of poverty are much higher among single mothers. This is the result of low wages for women coupled with few and expensive childcare facilities which force many single parents to stay on benefit. So the risks of poverty which accompany single parenthood are particularly acute for Caribbean women.

Some black people and other ethnic minorities are also more likely to live in homes with extended families. The Policy Studies Institute found that:

- 17% of Caribbean people and 22% of Asian people lived in households with more than three adults, compared with 6% of white people.[25]

The introduction of the poll tax – a flat-rate individual tax – has affected larger families particularly badly, and has, therefore, indirectly penalised black families. Government figures show that:

JUDY HARRISON/FORMAT

Every indicator of poverty shows that black people are more at risk of high unemployment, low pay, shift work, and poor social security rights than white people.

- 75% of families with three adults or more lose from the introduction of the poll tax compared to just 25% who have gained. [26]

Discrimination in social security

Mrs X has lived in the UK for many years and had been receiving supplementary benefit. In October 1980, she went to India for a visit and returned to the UK in July 1982. By the time she approached the take-up campaign at the end of December 1982, she had not received any benefit. She had received a letter from the DHSS which said: 'Please state below if there is anyone else in this country who can support you (friends or relatives) and also why you cannot return to India. Please also send your passport.'

(Passport to benefits: Racism in social security) [27]

The social security system discriminates both directly and indirectly against black people. Established after the Second World War, Beveridge's new welfare scheme assumed a homogenous society of white, UK-born, full-time male workers. It took no account of changing immigration patterns and the effect of these on entitlement to benefits.

Contributory benefits

Benefits such as retirement pension and unemployment benefit discriminate against people who are in intermittent and low-paid work. Anyone who earns *below* the national insurance threshold (currently £46 a week) does not make any contributions, and thereby does not receive any contributory benefits. As we have seen, black people are more likely to be both in low-paid work and more frequently unemployed. Such patterns affect their entitlement to all contributory benefits such as retirement pension. In addition, as many black people entered the scheme later in their working lives, they do not have enough contributions for the full retirement pension. They are therefore forced on to means-tested income support (formerly supplementary pension). Figures from the PSI show that fewer Asian and Caribbean than white people claimed retirement pension. Instead, a higher proportion of Caribbean people were dependent on supplementary pension (see p83).

Non-contributory benefits

These benefits have residence and/or presence conditions attached to them (see Table 15), some of which are more draconian than others. For example, to claim severe disablement allowance a claimant has to prove residence in the UK for 10 out of the preceding 20 years. Other non-contributory benefits such as child benefit were specifically aimed at people present in the UK. (Previously child tax allowances were payable for children supported outside the United Kingdom.)

Often families living in this country are still supporting other family members in their countries of origin. Since such obligations are not recognised by our social security system, this often means struggling to survive on much lower incomes:

> Out of my wages of £6 a week I used to send £3 a week back home. My weekly rent was £1.15 and the rest of my money, plus my husband's £6, went towards everything else, such as fares, food, bringing up the baby, raising the deposit on a house and saving for the fares to bring the three children over.

(The Heart of the Race) [28]

Means-tested benefits [29]

The link between benefits and immigration is explicit in the means-tested part of the social security system . As we saw on p84, for certain groups of people entry to the UK is dependent upon not relying on 'public funds'. The three main means-tested benefits all fall into this category. Claiming any one of these can either endanger the chances of bringing in the rest of the family or create problems for the sponsor. There is now a considerable body of evidence documenting the contact between the DSS and the Home Office. Passport checks on black claimants – regardless of whether they were born in the UK – have become a frequent occurrence at DSS offices.

Many reports have highlighted the low take-up of benefits amongst the black community. Fear of creating problems, concern that any fuss might affect residence, the lack of translated information, and no recognition by the DSS of any responsibility to provide interpreters have all created a climate in which black citizens are less likely to assert their rights, doubting their entitlement to benefits.

The radical overhaul of social security in 1988 accentuated the emphasis on means-testing and has meant greater hardship for black claimants:

- Entitlement to some premiums rests on receiving certain non-contributory benefits which are restricted by residence and/or presence tests.
- The lower rate of benefit for under 25s is indirectly discriminatory because black and other ethnic minority groups have a higher proportion of people who fall into this age-group.
- The social fund brings in discretion and no independent right of appeal and greater scope for racism. [30]
- Questions on the date of arrival in this country have been added to the income support form.

TABLE 15
Residence conditions for non-contributory benefits

Severe disablement allowance:
residence in the UK for 10 out of the previous 20 years
Invalid care allowance, attendance allowance:
residence in the UK for 26 weeks in the previous 52 weeks
Mobility allowance:
residence in the UK for 52 weeks in the previous 18 months
Non-contributory widows benefit and category C retirement pension:
resident for 10 years in the period 5 July 1948 - 1 November 1970 and
resident on 2 November 1970 or date of claim
Category D retirement pension:
resident in the UK for 10 years in the previous 20 years
Child benefit:
present in the UK for 6 months

Notes:
1. *The residence test for attendance allowance, invalid care allowance and mobility allowance is particularly strict – you have to be 'ordinarily resident' which requires some degree of continuity.*
2. *In addition to a residence test, generally people have to have been in Britain for a period of 6 months before claiming.*

These are only some of the difficulties that are caused by the new benefits system. In addition, the extension of means-testing exacerbates all the problems associated with the link between immigration status and entitlement to benefit. The further social security intrudes into the minutiae of individual circumstances the more room there is for racism. Some black people, excluded from all help under the new system, find themselves placed firmly in the category of the 'undeserving poor'.

Discrimination and racism

The legal framework for dealing with racism – beginning with the 1964 Race Relations Acts and strengthened by the 1976 Act – have had little impact on the levels of discrimination in employment.

In *Race Relations and Discrimination*[31], Colin Brown concludes:

> If what underlies employers' discriminatory actions is a bedrock of racial antipathy, then other recent events give few reasons to be optimistic about change for the better . . . it may be that the more subtle aspects of racial

inequality have been stressed too much, or too soon, while the main problem of British race relations is, plainly and simply, discrimination based on racial hostility.

Conclusion

Every indicator of poverty shows that black people and other ethnic minority groups are more at risk of high unemployment, low pay, shift work, and poor social security rights. Their poverty is caused by immigration policies which have often excluded people from abroad from access to welfare, employment patterns which have marginalised black people and other ethnic minority groups into low-paid manual work, direct and indirect discrimination in social security and the broader experience of racism in society as a whole.

Tackling poverty among black and ethnic minority groups is both about general policies for reducing poverty – such as reducing unemployment or introducing a minimum wage – and about specific policies. CPAG believes that the following specific policies would begin to reduce racial inequality:

- New employment opportunities and training programmes aimed at black and ethnic minority groups.
- Tougher anti-discriminatory measures in employment.
- The abolition of discriminatory aspects of the social security system.
- The translation of a wide variety of leaflets into minority languages, an obligation on the part of the Department of Social Security to provide interpreters, and take-up campaigns that specifically cater for the black and ethnic minority communities.
- A draft directive in Europe which forbids discrimination in social security (both in social assistance and insurance-based schemes) against ethnic minorities.
- The European Community Charter of Fundamental Human Rights should contain a commitment to ending racial inequality.

NOTES

1. K Amin and K Leech, 'A new "Underclass": race and poverty in the inner city', *Poverty 70*, CPAG Ltd, 1988.
2. *Households below Average Income 1981-1987*, DSS, 1990 and *Low Income Families* statistics 1985, DSS, 1988.

3. *Labour Force Surveys*, Department of Employment, published annually with a summary in the *Employment Gazette*.
4. C Brown, *Black and White Britain, the third PSI survey*, Policy Studies Institute, Gower, 1984.
5. Much of the material in this section comes from a forthcoming publication by K Amin with C Oppenheim, *Race and Poverty*, CPAG Ltd, 1990.
6. 'Ethnic Origin and the Labour Market', *Employment Gazette*, Department of Employment, March 1990.
7. S McRae, *Young and jobless*, Policy Studies Institute, 1987.
8. *Last among equals*, West Midlands Low Pay Unit, 1988.
9. *see* note 6.
10. *New Earnings Survey 1988*, Department of Employment, HMSO, 1989. We have used 1988 earnings figures for comparison with the Labour Force Survey.
11. *see* note 4.
12. *see* note 4.
13. B Bryan, S Dadzie, S Scafe, *The Heart of the Race*, Virago, 1985.
14. *see* note 4.
15. For full details on immigration policy, see P Gordon and F Klug, *British Immigration control: a brief guide*, Runnymede Trust, 1985.
16. C Brown, 'Race Relations and Discrimination' in *Policy Studies*, 11.2, PSI, Summer 1990.
17. *see* note 6.
18. *see* note 4.
19. R Penn, A Martin, and H Scattergood, *Employment Trajectories of Asian migrants in Rochdale: an integrated analysis*, Economic and Social Research Council, Working Paper 14, 1990.
20. *see* note 19.
21. T Ahmed and J Beliappa, *Computer access for Asians in the borough of Ealing: a focus on business and employment*, Confederation of Indian Organisations, London Voluntary Services Council, 1989.
22. C Benson, *An investigation of the access the black community has to employment and training in information technology*, London Voluntary Services Council, 1989.
23. *Social Trends 20*, 1990 edition, HMSO, 1990.
24. A Hadjipateras and S Slipman, *Helping one parent families to work*, National Council for One Parent Families, 1988.
25. *see* note 4.
26. Department of Employment press release, 15 February, 1988, Table 10.
27. P Gordon and A Newnham, *Passport to Benefits: Racism in social security*, CPAG Ltd and Runnymede Trust, 1985.
28. *see* note 13.
29. *see* note 27; and S Conlan, 'Without recourse to public funds: immigration and social security since the Second World War', unpublished dissertation, Leicester University, 1989.
30. *see* S Conlan, note 29.
31. *see* note 16.

SIX

Women and poverty

The simple fact is that throughout the last century women have always been much poorer than men. At the start of this century 61% of adults on all forms of poor relief were women.

Women and Poverty[1]

There is nothing new about women's poverty. Today 62% of adults supported by income support are women.[2]

Focusing on women's poverty raises crucial issues for the examination of poverty as a whole.[3] Caroline Glendinning's and Jane Millar's *Women and Poverty in Britain* brought together many of the central aspects of women's poverty. The authors argue that looking at women's risk of poverty is not simply a question of illuminating the disparate *levels* of income which exist between men and women. It is also about:

- their *access* to incomes and other resources; *and*
- the *time* spent in generating income and resources; *and*
- the *transfer* of these resources from some members of a household to others.

This approach facilitates a much more complex understanding of the nature of poverty which is not captured by straightforward statistics on family or household incomes.

Indicators of women's poverty

Low income

The major sources of data on poverty are not broken down by sex. Income is measured by the household or family unit. The *Low Income Families* Statistics and the Department of Social Security's figures – *Households below Average Income* – are no exception. However, it is possible to make a rough estimate of how many women are living in poverty by making assumptions about the number of women who are single parents, pensioners and so forth: [4]

- In 1987, approximately 4.5 million women, 3.2 million men and 2.5 million children were living in poverty (defined as on and below the supplementary benefit level).

Although the *Family Expenditure Survey* does not provide data about the incomes of men and women living in families, it does provide useful information about single person households broken down by sex. It shows that:

- in 1988, women's incomes were only 86% of men's;
- women in retirement were far more reliant on social security benefits than men, and were less likely to have annuities, pensions and investments (see Table 16);
- the greater reliance on social security in retirement by women is the outcome of lower earnings, intermittent work patterns, and fewer rights to occupational pensions. [5]

TABLE 16

Sources of income, single person households in 1988

| | Below pension age | | Above pension age | |
	Men aged under 65	Women aged under 60	Men aged over 65	Women aged over 60
Normal disposable weekly income	£156.16	£134.56	£91.91	£79.30
% of income from:				
Wages/salaries	72%	73%	–	3%
Investments	3%	5%	16%	13%
Annuities & pensions (not included under social security)	2%	4%	27%	19%
Social security benefits	6%	8%	46%	52%
Other	17%	10%	11%	13%

SOURCE: Family Expenditure Survey 1988, Table 22, HMSO, 1990

Research by Holly Sutherland at the London School of Economics has looked at the incomes of men and women in couples. Using a computer model of the tax and benefit system (Taxmod) she found that 9% of couples had incomes below the income support level. But looking at men and women separately within couples, she found that only 5% of husbands had incomes below half the income support level compared to a staggering 50% of wives. [6]

Low pay

I was earning roughly £35 to £40 a week. It was piece work, 13p per skirt – you had to sew hundreds to get to £35-£40 . . . I had to work sometimes until midnight, from nine in the morning, just to pay rent, electricity and gas.

(Sevin, mother of three) [7]

- In 1989, 6.34 million women were low paid – ie, 71% of the total number of people on low wages. The Low Pay Unit defines low pay as less than two-thirds of median male earnings – ie, earning less than £4.16 per hour or £157 per week, including overtime earnings. [8]
- There is a strong association between low pay and part-time work. In 1989, 4.28 million women worked part time and 79% of them were low paid. Only 0.89 million men worked part time with a slightly lower proportion who were low paid (72%).
- Many black women are likely to have even lower earnings and/or do more shift work (see Chapter 5):

Black people are in the lowest form of employment. When we came here in the fifties we went into work that white people wouldn't do. We got stuck in the lowest jobs.   (Valerie, single mother) [9]

- In 1989, average hourly earnings for women were 68% of men's (including overtime) and 76% (excluding overtime). [10]

Benefits

One of the main features of our social security system is the division between national insurance benefits and means-tested benefits. As long as sufficient contributions have been made, the former are paid on an individual basis regardless of income. Means-tested benefits are based on a test of income and capital however. Because women are more likely to have breaks in employment and to work part time and earn low wages, many fall below the threshold for making national insurance

contributions. In 1988, over 2 million women fell into this category. [11]
The result is that women forfeit their right to national insurance benefits.
Women are therefore less likely to have benefits in their own right than
men, and as a result are more dependent on the 'Cinderella' part of the
social security system – means-tested benefits.

In 1988: [12]

- over three times as many women over pension age – 1,190,000 –
  were receiving income support compared to 350,000 men;
- 727,000 single parents were reliant on income support – about
  two-thirds of all single parents;
- 96% of single parents on income support were women.

Exclusion

> Her father's always going on that he hasn't got any money and yet he's got a
> Cortina. I walk everywhere and I stay within this area.
>
> (Jenny, single mother) [13]

The indicators of poverty above look at hard facts, like wages and social
security. But there are less quantifiable aspects to poverty, like not being
able to go out for a drink or a meal, or missing out on seeing friends.
There is some evidence to show that this aspect of poverty is also different for men and women. A survey of 140 families living on supplementary benefit compared the activities pursued by men and women
on benefit. [14] It shows that while their activities outside the home were
severely curtailed by living on benefit, women, on the whole, were even
less likely to participate in such activities outside the home than men:

- 18% of men went out for a drink compared to 3% of women
- 18% of men took part in sport compared to 8% of women
- 11% of men went to the unemployed workers' centre while no
  women did.

On the other hand, women were far more likely to be cooking the main
meal or cleaning and dusting.

The causes of women's poverty

Women's lives are shaped by the family responsibilities they have traditionally taken on – the tasks of childcare, caring for the elderly and maintaining the home . These tasks shape women's work patterns, the type of occupations they work in, their earnings and their social security benefits. They push women into financial dependence upon men or upon state benefits. It is often assumed that women do not need an income of their own and that money, food and other resources are shared evenly within the family. For many women neither employment nor social security can keep them out of poverty.

Women's unpaid work

Women are responsible for the bulk of domestic work. *British Social Attitudes*, an annual survey, looked at the distribution of household tasks undertaken by men and women. [15] It found that the traditional division of labour is alive and kicking. In the period 1988-89:

- 50% of women were mainly responsible for shopping compared to 7% of men (the rest share);
- 77% of women were mainly responsible for making the evening meal (6% of men);
- 72% of women were mainly responsible for cleaning (4% of men);
- 88% of women were mainly responsible for washing and ironing (2% of men);
- 67% of women looked after children when sick (2% of men).

The only task that men were more likely to do than women was repairing household equipment – 82% of men were mainly responsible for this task compared to 6% of women.

Looking after children swallows up a large amount of time and is still usually done by women. A 1984 survey estimated that women were responsible for 48 hours out of 50 hours spent on basic childcare tasks. [16] More recently the London Living Standards Survey found that women with a child under 5 spent 65 hours a week on childcare compared to 20 hours spent by men. [17]

Caring for children has a knock-on effect on women's employment and earning capacity. Heather Joshi estimated that if a woman on average earnings had two children, she would lose £122,000 over a lifetime in lost earnings. This is the result of 8 years out of the labour market in the early years of having children, and working fewer hours and having lower earnings on return to work. [18] (This figure takes no account of the lower pension entitlement women are also likely to have.)

For parents bringing up children on their own the burden of childcare on a single wage is particularly difficult. The great majority of single parents are women (9 out of 10). Single parents are very dependent on social security for their income. The *Family Expenditure Survey 1988* shows the differences in the sources of income for a single parent in comparison with a couple: [19]

- on average 54% of the income for a single parent with one child was from earnings, and 34% from social security (the rest comes from self-employment, investments etc);
- for a single parent with two or more children the comparable figures were 32% from earnings and 44% from social security;
- on average 73% of the income for a couple with one child came from earnings, and 5% from social security;
- for a couple with two children the figures were 71% and 6% respectively.

Many single parents are forced to rely on benefit even though many would prefer to be in work because they are caught in the unemployment trap. Childcare facilities are few and far between and are often expensive. The part-time jobs on offer are often low paid. As a consequence, many single mothers have little choice but to stay on benefit for several years. As all the evidence shows, long-term reliance on benefit means hardship and very often debt (see pp54-7).

> I was very bitter. I was trying to help myself and I couldn't take a full-time job because the children and my husband had to be cared for. We had no transport and John couldn't get into a car, so that deprived us of going out anywhere. You watch other people going out to enjoy themselves and you feel so isolated . . . A woman is always caring . . . I mean who cares for carers?
>
> (Phyllis, who cares for her husband at home) [20]

It is not only caring for children that has a knock-on effect on women's lost earnings, but also caring for adult relatives who are elderly or sick or have a disability. In 1985 it was estimated that: [21]

- there were 6 million carers;
- 3.5 million women (15% of all women) were carers in comparison with 2.5 million men (12% of all men);
- the annual 'cost' of a woman giving up work in the late stages of life to care for an elderly person or someone with a disability (in terms of likely loss of income) was £8,500 for a woman with no

children, and £7,000 for a woman with children.[22] (The loss is lower for women with children because their earnings have already been depressed by having children);

- nearly half (45%) of all carers devoted 50 hours or more a week to caring.

Work at home, whether caring for the home or children or adults, is often neglected in any discussion of poverty. The amount of *time* spent trying to achieve a given standard of living – eg, cleaning, cooking and other forms of 'home production' – is an important aspect of poverty.[23] Jane Millar and Caroline Glendinning argue:

> The value of time – both in the generation of resources and in their use – has hitherto been largely ignored in poverty studies. If time were included it would almost certainly point out substantial differences between men and women.[24]

In other words, poverty is not just about income but about how income and other resources are generated and used. For example, it may take a woman on low pay 50 hours a week to earn an average wage – the amount of *time* trying to earn a living wage is an important aspect of her poverty. Another example is the amount of time it takes to do household tasks. Visits to the launderette, daily trips to the shops because there is never enough money for a big shop, making sandwiches because there isn't enough money for school dinners – all these absorb time. Not having sufficient money, or a washing machine, or a car, all mean that it takes much more time and work for someone in poverty to achieve the same standard of living as someone who is comfortably off.

Women's paid work

Women are far more likely to be working part time than men. The 1989 *Labour Force Survey* showed that:

- 77% of male employees worked full time and 4% part time;[25]
- 51% of female employees worked full time and 40% part time;
- 43% of married women employees worked full time and 48% part time.

> I think employers are hesitant to employ you full-time, knowing that you've got two young children. When I had Christopher, I didn't tell them I was a single parent. I did five nights a week, and Christopher went to my friend at nights and then I came home and looked after him in the day. I didn't know what living was about until I stopped doing night duty. I didn't see anybody.
>
> (Valerie, single mother)[26]

Patterns of part-time work are directly linked to responsibilities for caring for children or others. The *General Household Survey* publishes employment rates for women linking them to the age of their youngest child (see Table 17). It shows that as the youngest child gets older the mother is more likely to be in paid work. A majority of women with children in the youngest age group are not in paid work. [27]

TABLE 17

Employment rates for women of working age with children in 1987

	age of youngest child:		
	0–4	5–9	10+
% **working** full time	11%	14%	29%
part time	24%	48%	45%
% **not in paid work**	65%	38%	26%

SOURCE: *General Household Survey 1987, HMSO, 1990.*

Getting paid work is also intimately linked to the availability of childcare. The United Kingdom has one of the worst records of provision for publicly funded childcare places in the European Community. Only Luxembourg and Ireland have worse provision for under 2s and only Portugal less for 3- and 4-year-olds. In the United Kingdom only 2% of 0 to 2-year-olds and only 44% of over 3s were in publicly funded childcare places in 1985-86. [28] Compare this with 44% and 87% in Denmark. Even in poorer countries like Greece and Spain 62% and 66% respectively of 3-year-olds upwards were in publicly funded childcare:

> Childcare in this country is a joke. For a woman who has got very little resources unless you are lucky enough to get a government subsidised nursery, any private childcare is really expensive . . . that one factor stops a lot of women from coming off social security and getting a job.
>
> (Grace, single mother) [29]

Not only are women more likely to be in part-time work, but there is also a marked sexual division of labour. Women are much more likely to be working in: [30]

- education, welfare and health (14% of women compared to 5% of men in 1989);
- clerical work (30% of women compared to 6% of men in 1989);

- catering, cleaning, hairdressing and other personal services (21% of women compared to 4% of men in 1989);
- retail (10% of women compared to 5% of men in 1989).

Clerical work and catering work have a high proportion of low-paid workers. In 1989: [31]

- in education, welfare and health, 20% of the full-time female workforce earned under £160 a week;
- in clerical and related work, 56% of the full-time female workforce earned under £160 a week;
- in catering, cleaning, hairdressing and other personal services, 82% of the full-time female workforce earned below £160.
- in retail, 73% of the full-time female workforce earned below £160 a week.

TABLE 18

Percentage of jobs where employer provides benefits, by gender

	Male full-timers	Female full-timers	Female part-timers
pensions*	73	68	31
sick pay*	66	58	27
paid time off	64	48	30
unpaid time off	54	54	57
company car or van	30	10	5
free/subsidised transport	31	24	17
goods at a discount	47	40	31
free or subsidised meals	39	47	25
finance/loans	21	20	12
accommodation	14	17	5
life assurance	39	19	5
private health	31	22	9
recreation facilities	40	36	24
maternity pay	–	31	16
childcare	1	13	10

* above basic government scheme

SOURCE: *Unequal Jobs, Unequal Pay, ESRC, The Social Change and Economic Life Initiative, Working Paper 6, 1989*

Women are also far less likely to have access to occupational and fringe benefits at work. A recent study found that a lower proportion of full-time women workers had access to almost all types of benefit (after allowing for differences in skill and job content) in comparison with men. For part-time women workers this pattern was even more marked (see Table 18). [32]

Whose money?

> I won't touch jumble sales . . . I'll buy the cheapest for myself, or second hand, but not for the kids.
>
> (Molly, mother of six, living with husband who is registered disabled) [33]

> I'll go to jumble sales for my clothes . . . But I'm not seeing me kid and me husband walk to town with secondhand clothes on. I'll make do myself, but I won't make do for them. I wouldn't mind a new coat but I can't have one.
>
> (Emily, mother of three, husband unemployed) [34]

The distribution of money, food, and other goods inside the home is an area which is seen as *private* and is therefore very difficult to research. [35] The quotations above illustrate the ways in which women often put the needs of their families above their own. By impoverishing themselves women help to prevent or reduce poverty for other members of their family. [36] Jan Pahl's *Money and Marriage* looks at how money is handled inside the family. [37] The author shows that women in couples are likely to have less income of their own than men: 83% of women in couples had an income of less than £57 a week compared with 6% of men (the result of differential earnings, savings, gifts and child benefit). Pahl also found that in poorer households and in households in the North, North-West and in Wales, women are more likely to be responsible for the family budget. But holding the purse strings does not necessarily confer power:

> Women are responsible for family finances but they have none of the power that goes with possession. Having it in their hands never made money their own.   (Beatrix Campbell) [38]

The bulk of the money a woman brings into the home is spent on household consumption. Pahl also found that, as far as household spending was concerned, men contributed more in absolute terms and women contributed more in relative terms:

> Put simply, if a pound entered the household economy through the mother's hands more of it would be spent on food for the family than would be the case if the pound had been brought into the household by the father. [39]

In addition, Pahl found that husbands were more likely to have money for personal spending and leisure than the women:

- 44% of men compared to 28% of women had personal spending money;
- 86% of men and 67% of women spent money on leisure pursuits.

He liked cars and drinking and there wasn't the money for it. Me and the kids used to go short on food and clothes because he spent the money.

(Vanessa, single mother) [40]

He wanted extra money off me which I couldn't give him, which led to rows and then in the end I were saying there were only the £5 electricity money left and he were taking it and spending it. And then on Monday when I cashed the family allowance, he wanted money out of that as well. So that didn't help.

(Carol, single mother of three, expecting another) [41]

Conclusion

Women's poverty is compounded over a lifetime. Their lower rates of pay, work patterns interrupted because of caring for others, the trap of part-time work, and the diminished social security, occupational and private benefits received as a result of their work patterns combine to impoverish women throughout their lives. Women's longer life expectancy and their reduced access to pensions means that a high proportion are living out their lives on pitiful levels of income.

Many measures which help people living in poverty would benefit women in particular. CPAG believes that the following policies would begin to deal with the poverty faced by women:

- A statutory minimum wage for full- and part-time workers, and pro-rata employment rights for part-time workers.
- Improving the rights of parents in employment (eg, parental leave, paternity and maternity leave etc).
- A shorter working day and flexible hours of work.
- Steps towards a non-means-tested social security system without contribution conditions so that women with caring responsibilities would not be penalised for spending time out of the labour market.
- Individual entitlement to benefit.
- Increased availability of subsidised childcare.

NOTES

1. J Lewis and D Piachaud, 'Women and Poverty in Britain' in C Glendinning and J Millar, *Women and poverty in the twentieth century*, Wheatsheaf, 1987.
2. This is based on the following assumptions: in 1988 according to *Social Security Statistics* (HMSO, 1989) 2,420,000 women and 1,931,000 men received income support; 841,000 partners were provided for, 97% of whom are women. This makes a total of 3,236,000 women and 1,956,000 men provided for by income support.
3. J Millar and C Glendinning, 'Gender and poverty: a survey article', *Journal of Social Policy*, Vol 18, part 3, July 1989.
4. This figure assumes that 40% of single people under pension age are women; that 74% of single people over pension age are women; and that 96% of single parents on supplementary benefit are women (based on 1987 supplementary benefit statistics).
5. *Family Expenditure Survey 1988*, table 22, HMSO, 1990.
6. H Sutherland, forthcoming, quoted in AB Atkinson, *Poverty, Statistics and Progress in Europe*, revised version of keynote address at a seminar on Poverty Statistics in the EC, forthcoming publication in the Welfare State Programme, Suntory Toyota International Centre for Economics and Related Disciplines.
7. Quoted in 'Women and poverty' photographic exhibition, CPAG, 1986.
8. Low Pay Unit, Parliamentary briefing, No 1, 'Low Pay in Great Britain and the Regions', 8 March 1990.
9. *see* note 7.
10. *The New Review 1*, Low Pay Unit, 6 January 1990.
11. *House of Commons Hansard*, cols 531-2, 5 March 1990.
12. *Social Security Statistics 1989*, HMSO, 1989.
13. *see* note 7.
14. J Bradshaw and H Holmes, *Living on the edge: a study of the living standards of families on benefit living in Tyne and Wear*, Tyneside CPAG, 1989.
15. *British Social Attitudes*, 5th Report 1988/89, 'A woman's work', Social and Community Planning Research, Gower, 1988.
16. D Piachaud, *Round about 50 hours a week*, CPAG Ltd, 1984.
17. U Kowarzik and J Popay, *London Living Standards Survey*, 'Unpaid Work', unpublished paper, 1988.
18. H Joshi, 'The cash opportunity costs of childbearing', Centre for Economic Policy Research, Discussion Paper 208, 1988.
19. *Family Expenditure Survey* – *see* note 5.
20. *see* note 7.
21. H Green, *Informal carers, General Household Survey*, HMSO, 1988.
22. G Parker, *With due care and attention*, Family Policy Studies Centre, 1990.
23. D Piachaud, 'Problems in the Definition and Measurement of Poverty', *Journal of Social Policy*, Vol 116, part 2, April 1987.
24. *see* note 1.
25. *Employment Gazette*, 1989 Labour Force Survey: preliminary results, Department of Employment, April 1990.
26. *see* note 7.
27. *General Household Survey 1987*, Table 9.11, HMSO, 1989.
28. P Moss, *Childcare and equality of opportunity*, Commission of the European Communities, 1988.
29. *see* note 7.
30. *see* note 25.

31. *New Earnings Survey 1989*, HMSO, 1989.

32. S Howell, J Rubery, B Burchell, *Unequal Jobs, Unequal Pay*, Economic and Social Research Council, Working Paper 6, 1989.

33. G Craig and C Glendinning, quoted in *The impact of social security changes: the views of families living in disadvantaged areas*, Barnardos Research and Development, 1990.

34. *see* note 33.

35. See J Brannen and G Wilson (eds), *Give and take in families: studies in resource distribution*, Allen and Unwin, 1987.

36. *see* note 1.

37. J Pahl, *Money and Marriage*, Macmillan, 1989.

38. B Campbell, *Wigan Pier Revisited*, Virago, 1984

39. *see* note 37.

40. *see* note 33.

41. *see* note 33.

SEVEN

Poverty by region and country

The scene at Lime Street Station, Liverpool, around midnight on a bone-numbing Sunday had the time-warped feel of an old newsreel: a long line of shabbily-dressed men shuffling and stamping against the cold, stirring jerky black-and-white memories of civil upheaval, a stream of refugees.

But then these people are refugees, refugees from joblessness, making their weekly way to work in a place where they cannot afford to live, London.

These people work mostly in London's ever-lively building industry; a few work below stairs in the capital's hotels and restaurants. During the week they squat, live in huts on site or sleep in bed and breakfast joints in the East End and the inner suburbs. On Friday nights they take the train back to Liverpool for two days with their families before returning on the cheap fare midnight mail train.

Scousers: doing the South's dirty work [1]

The scale and nature of poverty depend partly on where you live. The rapid changes in our economic structure – in particular the decline of old industrial heartlands – have created distinctive regional and national patterns of unemployment and poverty. The North-South divide has dominated discussion of unemployment in Britain. There is some initial evidence to suggest that this divide is changing. A survey by the Confederation of British Industry showed more industrial capacity at work in the North than in the South for the first time in recent years. [2]

In addition, there are, of course, large differences *within* regions – eg, inner London suffers some of the worst levels of deprivation, but is within the affluent South-East. The figures we present below shed some light on the differences between nations and regions in the United Kingdom.

Poverty statistics

Northern Ireland is not a special case but a test case. No other region in the UK so clearly demonstrates that low wages, high unemployment and 'good' industrial relations are not the path to economic prosperity . . . No other region demonstrates so clearly the potential of social policies for integrating – or alienating minorities . . . Above all, no other region so effectively refutes the view that, over time, individuals, families and communities can adjust to poverty line incomes and unemployment and find ways of coping with the financial, social and psychological costs of income deprivation and worklessness.   (*On the Edge: a Study in Poverty*)[3]

Households below Average Income statistics, now the main official source of information on low income, do not provide data broken down by regions and nations.[4] In addition, the figures only refer to Britain and therefore exclude one of the areas of the most extreme levels of poverty – Northern Ireland. However, the Social Services Select Committee commissioned the Institute for Fiscal Studies to do a regional analysis of the *Households below Average Income* statistics. The analysis is for the years 1980-82 and 1983-85 (this is because the samples are small and so have to be pooled over the years). 1987 figures are not yet available.[5] **Throughout this chapter we have defined poverty as below 50% of average income.**

Table 19 shows that Northern Ireland ranks as the poorest area with 27% of its population living in poverty in 1983-5. The North, North-West, Yorkshire and Humberside and West Midlands follow with between 15% and 18% of their populations living in poverty. By contrast, the South-East has only 7%. In most regions and nations there was a rise in the proportion living in poverty between 1980-82 and 1983-85, with the exception of the South-East where they fell by 1%, and Yorkshire and Humberside and East Anglia where they remained constant. Wales and Scotland had higher proportions of people living in poverty than in England.

A higher proportion of children live in poverty than is the case with the population as a whole. For example in Northern Ireland in the period 1983-85, it is estimated that a staggering 39% – nearly 2 in 5 children – were living in poverty (see Table 20).

The major source of information about regional and national inequalities is *Regional Trends*, produced annually by the government's Central Statistical Office.[6] With statistics covering 1987-88, it provides the most

TABLE 19
Numbers and proportions of individuals living in poverty (below 50% of national average income) by region in 1980-82 and 1983-85. Based on household income after housing costs

	1980-82		1983-85	
	Nos (000s)	%	Nos (000s)	%
Northern	473	14	598	18
Yorkshire & Humberside	738	15	803	15
North-West	832	13	990	16
East Midlands	373	10	458	11
West Midlands	612	12	815	15
East Anglia	223	11	216	11
Greater London	538	9	635	12
South-East	791	8	710	7
South-West	358	9	408	10
England	4,995	11	5,510	12
Wales	398	13	426	14
Scotland	590	12	634	13
Northern Ireland	373	25	413	27
UK	6,300	11.5	7,090	12.8

Note: Figures do not add up exactly due to rounding.
SOURCE: Social Services Committee, Households below Average Income 1980-85: a regional analysis, HMSO, 1990, 378-I, Table C3

recent estimate of the distribution of household income. Similar patterns of inequalities between areas emerge (see Table 21). In Northern Ireland and the North nearly one-third (33%) of the population had an income of under £100 per week in 1987/88. In Scotland the figure was 30%. The South-East and South-West had a lower proportion of 18% and 19% respectively. At the top end of the income distribution, nearly a third (31%) of households in the South-East had incomes of above £400 a week. Meanwhile in Wales, only 13% of households had an income of £400 a week or more; Northern Ireland, Yorkshire and Humberside and the East Midlands follow with just 14%.

TABLE 20
Numbers and proportions of children living in poverty (below 50% of national average income) by region in 1980-82 and 1983-85. Based on household income after housing costs

	1980-82		1983-85	
	Nos (000s)	%	Nos (000s)	%
Northern	162	21	199	28
Yorkshire & Humberside	283	23	277	22
North-West	288	18	365	25
East Midlands	122	13	140	15
West Midlands	192	15	268	20
East Anglia	69	13	63	15
Greater London	161	12	203	19
South-East	290	12	245	10
South-West	101	11	141	15
England	1,653	15	1,904	18
Wales	122	17	173	23
Scotland	227	18	215	19
Northern Ireland	181	37	187	39
United Kingdom	2,200	16	2,480	19

Note: Figures do not add up exactly due to rounding.
SOURCE: Households below Average Income – A regional analysis 1980-85, Social Services Select Committee, HMSO 378-I, Table C7

Employment and unemployment

The structure of employment has changed radically in recent years with a major shift away from traditional manufacturing industry. This is the explanation for the persistence of higher rates of unemployment in regions and countries which were centres of manufacturing industry. [7]

- In the United Kingdom, manufacturing accounted for 23% of all employment in 1989, down from 31% in 1979.
- The Midlands and the North, North-West, Yorkshire and Humberside had the highest concentration of employment in manufacturing in 1979 (between a third and nearly half were in manufacturing).

TABLE 21
Distribution of household income 1987/88

| | Percentage of households in each weekly income group (per week) | | | Average Income £s per person |
	Under £100	£100-£400	£400+	
North	32	54	14	88
Yorks & Humberside	29	58	14	93
North-West	28	54	18	98
East Midlands	24	62	14	96
West Midlands	27	57	16	93
East Anglia	24	60	16	105
South-East	18	51	31	136
South-West	19	63	18	109
England	24	56	21	111
Wales	26	61	13	85
Scotland	30	55	15	95
Northern Ireland	32	55	14	74
United Kingdom	24	56	20	107

Note: Figures do not add up exactly due to rounding.
SOURCE: Regional Trends 25, 1990 Edition, HMSO, 1990, table 11.2

- New industries such as banking, finance, insurance and business services have increased from 7% to 12% of total employment over the same period. The rise of the new industries has been much more pronounced in the South-East and South-West than in the traditional manufacturing strongholds.

In other words, those areas that have been most impoverished by the dismantling of manufacturing industries have also gained least from the development of new forms of employment.

Not surprisingly, regional and national inequalities are reflected in patterns of unemployment and the distribution of earnings. In 1989, Northern Ireland had the worst unemployment rate at 15%, which was followed by the North with 10% (see Map A).[8] Table 22 shows that as unemployment as a whole grew, the disparity between different regions also grew. For example, the difference between the unemployment rate

JOHN STURROCK/NETWORK

The last ship launched from Smiths Dock, near Middlesborough...Those areas which have been most impoverished by the decline of manufacturing have also gained least from the development of new forms of employment.

in the North and the South-East was 1.5% in 1966; twenty years later, at the height of unemployment, it was 7.1% and by 1989 it had gone down slightly to 6.1%.

A higher proportion of the population earn low wages in the poorer regions – in 1989 in Northern Ireland 41% of men earned below £180 per week, followed by Wales with 33%. In the South-East just 19% earned below this level. [9]

TABLE 22
Unemployment rates in 1966, 1976, 1986 and 1989, by region

| | unemployment rate | | | |
| | 1966 | 1976 | 1986 | 1989 |
	%	%	%	%
North	2.4	5.3	15.4	10.0
Yorkshire & Humberside	1.1	3.9	12.6	7.7
North-West	1.4	5.1	13.8	8.4
East Midlands	1.0	3.5	9.9	6.2
West Midlands	0.8	4.3	12.6	6.7
East Anglia	1.4	3.5	8.1	4.4
South-East	0.9	3.1	8.3	3.9
South-West	1.7	4.7	9.5	4.5
England	–	3.9	11.3	6.2
Wales	2.7	5.3	13.9	7.8
Scotland	2.7	5.1	13.4	9.3
Northern Ireland	–	7.1	17.4	15.1
United Kingdom	–	4.2	11.2	6.3
Britain	1.4			

SOURCE: *Regional Trends, Table 10.19, HMSO, 1990 Edition, and Employment Gazette, Department of Employment, June 1973*

London

Just across the marshes of the Lea Valley from Hackney lies Lea Bridge Industrial Estate . . . By 1981 the place, like so much of British manufacturing industry, was coming to resemble the aftermath of a neutron bomb . . . with the people gone but the buildings still left standing. As all over Hackney,

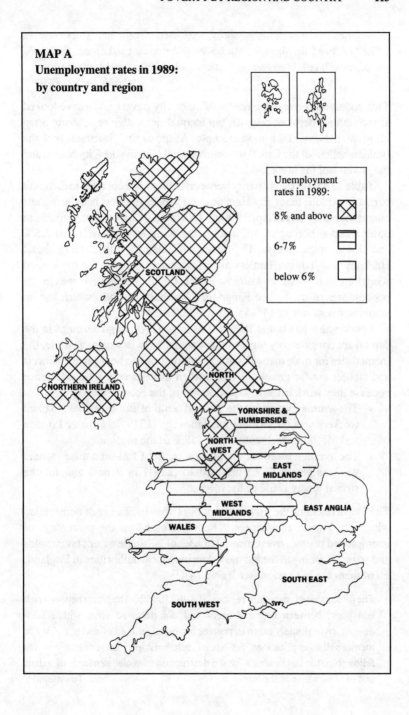

MAP A
Unemployment rates in 1989:
by country and region

Unemployment
rates in 1989:

8% and above

6-7%

below 6%

SCOTLAND

NORTHERN IRELAND

NORTH

YORKSHIRE &
HUMBERSIDE

NORTH
WEST

EAST
MIDLANDS

WEST
MIDLANDS

EAST ANGLIA

WALES

SOUTH EAST

SOUTH WEST

factories that once produced shoes, steel sheets, cords and cables bore 'To Let' or 'For Sale' signs . . . Machinery gathered dust and rusted, roofs leaked, paint flaked. Idle plant here, idle workers signing on the dole there.

(Inside the Inner City) [10]

This quotation conveys the nature of inner city poverty. We have looked at inequalities between regions, but inequalities *within* regions are often far greater. London is a good example. As the capital, it attracts both the 'golden hellos' of the City (large bonuses paid during the City boom) and the poverty of the homeless.

Table 23 shows the disparity between unemployment rates in different parts of London. Inner city Hackney and Tower Hamlets had the highest unemployment rates in April 1990 – 13.9% and 13.4%. Compare this to outer London boroughs, Hillingdon and Kingston, where it was 2.5% and 2.4% respectively. The levels of unemployment which beset Hackney and Tower Hamlets are over double the rate for the United Kingdom as a whole and almost match the unemployment rate in the poorest area of the United Kingdom – Northern Ireland – which had an unemployment rate of 14% in April 1990 (see Map B).

London also has larger inequalities in pay. Although earnings in the capital are considerably higher on average than in Britain as a whole, the inequalities for male manual workers within London between the poorest and richest are far greater. [11] For women there is very little difference because they work in the low-paid sector of the economy:

- The average wage for the poorest tenth of full-time male manual workers was 63% of the median wage (£219) in Greater London and for the richest tenth it was 158% of the median.
- The average wage for the poorest tenth of full-time male manual workers was 80% of the median (£161) in Britain and for the richest it was 126% of the median.

The Department of the Environment publishes indicators of deprivation which are known as z-scores. These are based on the percentage of unemployed people, overcrowded households, single parent households and so on. Looking at the ten most deprived local authorities in England, *all* of them are in London (see Table 24): [12]

The divide that exists within regions, the divide within the North between rich and poor, between deprived areas and non-deprived areas within London . . . (is) infinitely more important for us to get hold of and to . . . try to measure the implications for social relationships, the implications for fellowship, the implications for the destruction of social standards of values and of observance of the law.   (Peter Townsend) [13]

MAP B

Unemployment in Greater London, 1989

1 ISLINGTON
2 HACKNEY
3 TOWER HAMLETS
4 SOUTHWARK
5 CITY
6 WESTMINSTER
7 KENSINGTON & CHELSEA
8 HAMMERSMITH & FULHAM

Unemployment
rates in 1989:

10% & above

7-9%

below 7%

SOURCE: Updated table from Regional Policy: The North-South Divide, Paul Balchin, Paul Chapman Publishing Ltd, 1990

TABLE 23
Unemployment rates of London boroughs in April 1990 (percentages)

	Dept of Employment Index	Unemployment Unit Index
Barking & Dagenham	4.9	7.5
Barnet	3.5	5.3
Bexley	3.7	5.7
Brent	6.3	9.8
Bromley	3.1	4.8
Camden	7.8	11.3
Croydon	3.8	5.9
Ealing	4.5	6.8
Enfield	4.8	7.3
Greenwich	7.8	11.9
Hackney	13.9	21.3
Hammersmith & Fulham	7.9	11.6
Haringey	11.2	17.2
Harrow	2.5	3.8
Havering	2.6	4.1
Hillingdon	2.3	3.6
Hounslow	3.9	5.9
Islington	10.9	16.2
Kensington & Chelsea	5.2	7.6
Kingston	2.4	3.5
Lambeth	10.4	16.0
Lewisham	8.6	13.4
Merton	3.7	5.5
Newham	10.4	15.9
Redbridge	3.7	5.6
Richmond	2.6	3.7
Southwark	10.6	16.3
Sutton	2.7	4.0
Tower Hamlets	13.4	20.4
Waltham Forest	6.8	10.1
Wandsworth	5.9	9.0
Westminster	5.0	7.3
UK	5.6	8.4

SOURCE: Unemployment Unit Briefing: Unemployment: Totals & Rates in Parliamentary Constituencies, April 1990

TABLE 24
The ten most deprived English authorities ranked in order of deprivation, by z score (the Department of Environment's indicators of deprivation)

Hackney	6.69
Newham	5.84
Tower Hamlets	5.53
Lambeth	5.52
Hammersmith	4.98
Haringey	4.86
Islington	4.80
Brent	4.62
Wandsworth	4.50
Southwark	4.40

SOURCE: *A Charge on the Community, P Esam and C Oppenheim, CPAG Ltd and LGIU, 1989*

Conclusion

A series of new geographical boundaries has come to divide the United Kingdom, marking off the affluent regions and countries from the poorest. Northern Ireland ranks as the poorest on all counts – unemployment, poverty, and low incomes. The survey by the Institute for Fiscal Studies found that the North, North-West, Yorkshire and Humberside and the West Midlands had the largest proportions of their populations living in poverty, after Northern Ireland. Meanwhile the South-East, South-West and East Anglia fared rather better. Wales and Scotland had slightly higher proportions of people in poverty than in England. However, it should be borne in mind that this broad brush approach to regional inequality also masks vast differences within regions. For example, the lower unemployment and greater affluence in East Anglia hides the rural poverty of agricultural workers who have always been paid low wages; the highest average income in the South-East masks the acute pockets of poverty in Inner London.

NOTES

1. C Nevin, 'Scousers: doing the South's dirty work', *Daily Telegraph*, 19 January 1987.
2. I Hamilton Fazey, 'The North-South divide begins to close', *Financial Times*, 10 September 1990.
3. E Evason, *On the edge: a study of poverty and long-term unemployment in Northern Ireland*, CPAG Ltd, 1985.
4. *Households below Average Income – a regional analysis 1980-1985*, Social Services Select Committee, HMSO, 1990, 378-I.
5. *see* note 4.
6. Central Statistical Office, *Regional Trends 25*, 1990 Edition, HMSO, 1990.
7. *see* note 6.
8. *see* note 6.
9. *see* note 6.
10. P Harrison, *Inside the Inner City*, Penguin, 1983.
11. *New Earnings Survey 1989*, Part E, HMSO, 1989.
12. P Esam and C Oppenheim, *A charge on the community*, CPAG Ltd and LGIU, 1989.
13. P Townsend, 'The Scandal of Divided London', lecture to the London Churches Group, 1986.

EIGHT

Poverty in other countries

The prospect of the single internal market will generate a higher rate of economic growth, but unless the Community takes appropriate action and mobilises its resources more effectively, poverty will continue to exist.

Interim Report, Commission of the European Communities [1]

In 1985 one in seven people in the European Community (EC) were living in poverty. [2] How does the United Kingdom compare with its European partners? This is not just an academic question. The coming of the single European market in 1992 will bring significant economic and social changes which will reshape patterns of poverty and inequality within the Community. In the light of such an upheaval it becomes even more important to look at poverty in relation to our neighbours in order to assess how far we are experiencing common or differing trends, and to gauge the impact of a free market in Western Europe on our societies. **Throughout this chapter, poverty is defined as less than 50% of average income.**

The countries of the EC are very different, ranging from highly industrialised Germany to countries like Greece, Ireland, Portugal and Spain which have large agricultural sectors. There are also considerable disparities in wealth: Luxembourg has the highest per capita gross domestic product, and Portugal the lowest, both in relation to the European average (see Table 25). These characteristics shape the nature of poverty in the different countries. There are also large differences within countries. For example, in the Southern region of Italy double the proportion of the workforce is in low-paid agricultural work – 19.3% – in comparison with 9.8% in Italy as a whole. The Gross Domestic Product per capita in this region is 68% of the average for the EC, while Italy as a whole has 104% of the average for the EC. [3]

TABLE 25
European Communities Comparisons: Gross Domestic Product
(per head)

Country	
European Community	100
Belgium	101
Denmark	109
France	109
West Germany	113
Greece	55
Ireland	65
Italy	104
Luxembourg	121
Netherlands	103
Portugal	54
Spain	75
United Kingdom	107

Note: GDP per head is compared to the European Community average.
SOURCE: Regional Trends 25, 1990, Table 14.1, HMSO, 1990

Poverty in the industrialised West

It is the poorest countries which have the highest rates of poverty. The latest survey shows comparative rates of poverty in the EC in 1985.[4] Table 26 and Map C set out the proportions and numbers of the population in poverty in each country. Poverty is defined as less than 50% of the national average disposable income, adjusted for family size. This is not a poverty standard which is the same across the EC but one which varies from country to country.

In 1985:

- Greece and Portugal had the worst rates of poverty – around a quarter of their population was living in poverty;
- Ireland and Spain followed with a fifth of their population in poverty;
- in France one in six (18%) were poor and in Denmark between one in seven or eight (15%) were poor;

TABLE 26

Poverty rates and numbers 1973-77 and 1984-85 (persons)

		%	Nos (000s)
Belgium	1976	7.9	773.3
	1985	7.2	705.9
Denmark	1977	12.4	614.9
	1985	14.7	750.0
France	1975	19.9	10,173.5
	1985	17.5	9,375.6
West Germany	1973	8.8	5,238.2
	1985	8.5	5,026.7
Greece	1974	26.6	2,290.2
	1985	24.0	2,280.0
Ireland	1973	16.4	486.6
	1985	22.0	770.0
Italy	1975	10.6	5,861.1
	1984	11.7	6,678.4
Luxembourg	1975	7.9	31.5
	1985	7.9	31.5
Netherlands	1977	6.6	898.8
	1985	7.4	1,058.2
Portugal	1973/74	23.4	1,793.0
	1985	28.0	2,851.8
Spain	1973	20.0	6,794.5
	1985	20.0	7,701.0
United Kingdom	1975	6.7	3,624.7
	1985	12.0	6,636.0
Total	1973/77	12.8	38,580.3
	1984/85	13.9	43,865.1

Note: Poverty is defined as less than 50% of average equivalent disposable income for each country.

- the UK and Italy had around 12 % of the population (just below the average for the EC) in poverty. (It is important to note that the figure quoted here for the UK differs from the figure from *Households below Average Income*, as different assumptions are made); [5]

- Belgium, Germany, the Netherlands and Luxembourg had the lowest rates of poverty – between 7% and 8% of the population.

One very striking change in recent years is the sharp increase in poverty in Ireland and the United Kingdom between 1975 and 1985. During this period, the UK had the sharpest rise in poverty in the EC, nearly doubling between 1975 and 1985. Meanwhile, in Belgium, West Germany, Luxembourg and Spain, poverty rates stayed relatively constant over the period. In France and Greece the levels of poverty declined slightly. *Thus the situation in the UK deteriorated, while the rest of Europe either maintained the status quo or reduced its poverty levels.*

These figures are based on a *national* poverty line. Recent research by Tony Atkinson compares the pattern of poverty using both the *national* definition of poverty (as above) and a *Community wide* definition of poverty.[6] He sets the latter at 50% of the European Community average income and demonstrates:

- using a *Community-wide* definition, the overall poverty rate is 17.4%; it is 13.9% using a *national* definition (see above);
- using a *Community-wide* definition, Spain, Ireland, Greece and Portugal account for 55% of those in poverty; they account for 32% using a *national* definition.

Atkinson also looks at the effect of economic growth on the levels of poverty both between different European countries and within European countries.[7] He concludes:

> The crucial effects of growth are likely to be the impact on the distribution [of income] within countries. This obviously depends crucially on policy decisions, at national and Community level. It depends on the form that economic growth takes, including the regional pattern, and on the extent of harmonisation in areas such as minimum income provisions. Here I will simply make the point that *one cannot rely on growth itself being equalising in its impact*.
>
> (our emphasis)

The Luxembourg Income Study (LIS) looks at poverty and inequality in a number of countries inside and *outside* Europe.[8] Although the data are old, they demonstrate the effectiveness of cash benefits and direct tax in different countries to reduce poverty in 1979. Poverty is defined as half of median income adjusted for family size (see Definitions and Terms). LIS found that in 1979:

- the highest rates of poverty were in the United States (17%), Israel (15%), and Canada (12%); the lowest were in the Scandinavian countries (5%); and West Germany (6%) and the United Kingdom

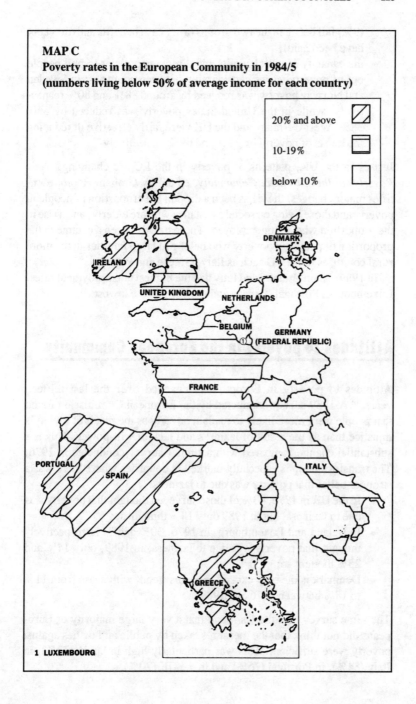

MAP C
Poverty rates in the European Community in 1984/5
(numbers living below 50% of average income for each country)

20% and above

10-19%

below 10%

DENMARK

IRELAND

UNITED KINGDOM

NETHERLANDS

BELGIUM

GERMANY
(FEDERAL REPUBLIC)

FRANCE

PORTUGAL

SPAIN

ITALY

GREECE

1 LUXEMBOURG

(9%) fall between the two groups (after cash benefits and direct tax have been paid);
- the capacity of cash benefits and direct tax policies to pull people out of poverty varies considerably between countries: in Sweden and Norway poverty was reduced by around 88% and 80% respectively, while in the United States poverty was reduced by only 38%. West Germany and the UK were fairly effective in reducing the levels of poverty by 79% and 69% respectively.

Just as in the UK, patterns of poverty in the EC are changing. *'New Poverty' in the European Community*, edited by Graham Room, identifies major changes: there has been a drop in the proportion of people in poverty and those living on social assistance who are elderly, and a rise in the proportion who are unemployed. There has also been a decline in the proportion of people in poverty who belong to large families in the more rural countries in the EC such as Italy, Greece and Portugal. [9]

In 1989, Spain, Ireland and Italy had the highest unemployment rates. Luxembourg, Portugal, Greece and the UK had the lowest.

Attitudes to poverty in the European Community

Attitudes to poverty in Europe have changed over the last thirteen years. [10] A 1989 survey conducted by the European Commission found that people were more likely to explain poverty as the result of society's injustice than as the result of laziness and lack of will-power. This is a substantial change compared with a similar survey conducted in 1976. The transformation is especially marked in countries where there was a stronger belief that poverty was due to laziness:
- In the UK in 1976, 43% of those surveyed thought that poverty was due to laziness, but in 1989 only 18% thought so;
- In Ireland and Luxembourg, in 1976, 30% and 31% respectively thought that poverty was due to laziness; in 1989, only 14% and 25% thought so;
- Denmark is the only exception to this trend, with a rise from 11% to 18% between 1976 and 1989.

The same survey of attitudes found that a very large majority of Europeans did not think that the measures taken by public authorities against poverty were sufficient. This was particularly high in Spain (77%), in Italy (84%), in Portugal (76%) and in the UK (70%).

Conclusion

The United Kingdom experienced an unparallelled rise in poverty between the mid-seventies and mid-eighties in comparison with its neighbours in the European Community. In relation to selected industrialised countries in 1979, the United Kingdom fell into the middle group with West Germany; poverty rates were worse in the United States, Canada and Israel and better in the Scandinavian countries. The approach of 1992 and the upheavals in Eastern Europe herald important changes within this region of the world – shifting industry, employment, wealth and poverty both between and within countries. It is essential that we monitor the impact of these changes on those living in or on the margins of poverty.

CPAG believes that the 'social dimension' of the 1992 European single market should be strengthened, and that in particular the UK should;

- endorse the European draft directives on parental leave and leave for family reasons, and on pro-rata rights for part-time workers and temporary workers;
- propose draft directives on: a minimum wage, a guaranteed minimum income, discrimination in social security against ethnic minorities and against unemployed people, minimum standards of provision for childcare services;
- support a systematic and published analysis of poverty country by country;
- support the creation of an all-party anti-poverty group in the European Parliament to monitor changes in poverty.

NOTES

1. *Interim report on a specific community action programme to combat poverty*, Commission of the European Communities, 1989.
2. M O'Higgins and Dr S Jenkins, 'Poverty in Europe: estimates for 1975, 1980 and 1985', unpublished paper, August 1989.
3. Central Statistical Office, *Regional Trends 25, 1990*, Table 14.1, HMSO, 1990.
4. *see* note 2.
5. *Households below Average Income* relate to Britain, while the European figures relate to the United Kingdom; the equivalence scales used are also different (see A B Atkinson for further information; note 6).
6. A B Atkinson, 'Poverty statistics and progress in Europe', revised keynote address on poverty, forthcoming publication in the Welfare State Programme, Suntory Toyota International Centre for Economics and Related Disciplines.

7.   *see* note 6.
8.   T H Smeeding, M O'Higgins, L Rainwater, (eds), *Poverty, inequality and income distribution in comparative perspective: the Luxembourg income study*, Wheatsheaf, 1990.
9.   G Room, *New poverty in the European Community*, Macmillan Press, forthcoming, November 1990.
10. *The perception of poverty in Europe*, Poverty 3, Eurobarometer, Commission of the European Communities, 1990.

NINE

Poverty in a wealthy society

To describe British society as one of public squalor and private affluence is to resort to an apt if well-worn cliché. Yet the fact remains that whatever the favoured slogan, the evidence is stark – the divide between rich and poor has grown ever wider. Some believe that such a divide is irrelevant as long as overall standards of living improve. But for CPAG, along with many others, such divisions scar our society. As former Conservative Minister Lord Alport wrote in 1985[1]: 'Britain as a nation is becoming increasingly divided, anxious and embittered.'

Indicators of division between rich and poor

According to the regular surveys conducted by *Economic Trends*[2] the earlier distribution from rich to poor has been put into reverse. The statistics reveal that in recent years household income has not trickled down but filtered up from the poorer sections of society to the richer ones.

Table 27 shows how the total amount of income held by households is distributed between the richest and poorest fifths of society. Two measures of income are used: 'original income' (ie, income before any taxes and benefits have been paid) and 'post-tax income' (ie, income after direct and indirect taxes and cash benefits). Households are divided into fifths from bottom to top; these are known as *quintile* groups.

Between 1977 and 1987:

- the poorest fifth's share of total original income halved from 0.6% to 0.3%;
- the richest fifth's share of original income went up by 7 percentage points from 44% to 51%;
- the poorest fifth's share of all post-tax income has gone down from 6.4% to 5.1%;
- the richest fifth's share of all post-tax income has grown from 40% to 45%;

TABLE 27

Percentage distribution of total original and post-tax income of households, broken down into quintile groups

Original Income	1977 %	1979 %	1987 %
Quintile group			
Bottom	0.6	0.5	0.3
2nd	10	9	6
3rd	19	19	16
4th	27	27	27
Top	44	45	51
Post-tax income			
Quintile group			
Bottom	6.4	6.1	5.1
2nd	12	11	10
3rd	18	18	16
4th	24	25	24
Top	39	40	45

* Income is not adjusted to take account of family size.
SOURCE: Economic Trends, May 1990, HMSO, 1990

In fact, most of this shift from poor to rich occurred after 1979. The share of the top fifth in 1987 after taxes and cash benefits (45%) is now the same as it was in 1979 before any taxes and cash benefits had been paid.

For the first time, *Economic Trends* has published data which adjust income for family size ('equivalising' income as it is known – see Definitions and Terms). [3] However, as yet it has not produced any data on a comparable basis over time (this will appear in 1991).

The share of total household income is slightly less unequal when income is adjusted for family size (see *fig* 9). The effect of changing the measure of income also changes who falls into the different quintile groups, pushing more families with children into the poorest fifth. In 1987, 48% of the poorest fifth was composed of retired households; 19% of two-parent family households; 9% of one-parent family households; 15% of one- or two-adult households; and the remainder were three-adult households.

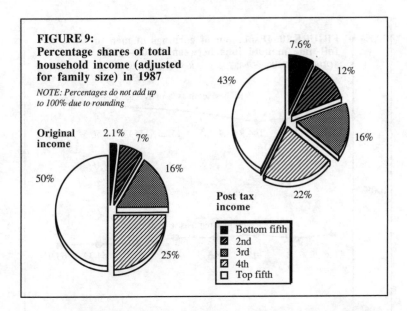

FIGURE 9:
Percentage shares of total household income (adjusted for family size) in 1987

NOTE: Percentages do not add up to 100% due to rounding

Original income

Post tax income

Bottom fifth
2nd
3rd
4th
Top fifth

One of the mainstays of government policy has been the the creation of a 'share-owning democracy' and a society of home owners. As part of this policy a number of public assets – such as telephones, gas, water and so on – have been privatised. Who owns these shares?[4]

In 1987:

- 13% of all share-owners were in professional occupations; 30% in managerial occupations; 23% in intermediate and junior non-manual occupations; 23% in skilled manual occupations; 8% in semi-skilled occupations; and just 2% in unskilled occupations;
- share ownership increases with rising income: only 10% of people with a gross weekly income of £50 or less (mainly pensioners) owned shares, and 15% of people with a gross weekly income of £50-£100; while 67% of people with a weekly income of £450 or more owned shares.

As the figures show, inequalities of share ownership simply mirror the inequalities of income.

Pay inequality

The last decade has been characterised by a substantial rise in earnings. However, the improvement of living standards for the average person masks a growing gap between the highest and lowest paid.[5]

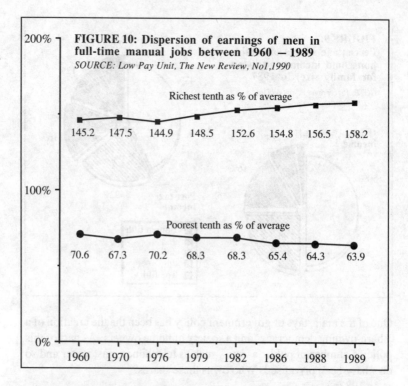

200% ┐ **FIGURE 10: Dispersion of earnings of men in full-time manual jobs between 1960 – 1989**
SOURCE: *Low Pay Unit, The New Review, No1,1990*

Richest tenth as % of average

145.2   147.5   144.9   148.5   152.6   154.8   156.5   158.2

100% ─

Poorest tenth as % of average

70.6   67.3   70.2   68.3   68.3   65.4   64.3   63.9

0% ─

1960   1970   1976   1979   1982   1986   1988   1989

- In 1979, the poorest tenth of men in full-time manual work earned 68% of the average wage and the richest tenth earned 149%.
- In 1989, the poorest tenth earned 64% of the average wage and the richest tenth 158% of the average.

Fig 10 shows how the pattern developed over almost thirty years.

High earnings are difficult to measure because a significant proportion of income comes in the form of bonuses etc, and is thus hidden. A survey published in the *Financial Times* under the headline 'Why people can be paid more than is good for anyone' shows top City of London salaries. [6] While only a minority of people earn such sums of money, it is an indicator of some of the lavish incomes that have characterised what until recently has been a booming financial sector. The top four positions in the City had the following salaries and bonuses:

- *Treasury head, big bank*: average salary £217,658, average bonus 69.4%, company car with an average price of £22,125;
- *General manager, big*: average salary £148,213, average bonus 30.1%, company car with an average price of £22,000;

JOHN STURROCK/NETWORK

'The cuts in direct taxes have been entirely paid for by the cuts in the generosity of benefits. The overwhelming majority of the bottom half have lost; the overwhelming majority of the top 30% have gained.'

- *Capital markets head*: average salary £122,021, average bonus 21.6%, company car with an average price of £19,600;
- *General manager medium*: average salary £101,320, average bonus 22.8%, company car with an average price of £21,500.

Taxation and social security policies

There have been substantial reductions in income tax for people living on higher incomes in the 1980 and 1988 Budgets. If the 1978/79 tax system were in place today, £27 billion more tax revenue would be raised. Who has benefited from this £27 billion?[7]

- 2.9 million tax-payers earning under £5,000 have gained an average of £110 a year or £480 million in total – 2% of the total tax cuts.
- 6.4 million tax-payers earning between £10,000 and £15,000 have gained an average of £690 a year, or £4,390 million in total – 16% of the total tax cuts.
- A mere 0.2 million tax-payers at the very top end of the income distribution with earnings of £70,000 or more have gained £36,060 a year, or £5,770 million in total – 21% of the total tax cuts.

In *Changing Tax*, John Hills analyses the effect of changes in taxation and social security since 1979.[8] He shows the differences between the 1988/89 tax and social security system and those that would have resulted if the 1978/89 system had been uprated with the subsequent rise in national income. It reveals the way in which government policies have sharply increased the division between rich and poor:

- the bottom 50% lost nearly £8.50 a week;
- the top 10% gained nearly £40 a week;
- 57% of families lost and 40% gained.

As John Hills concludes:

Remarkably, what has happened has been a virtually zero net cost reform: the cuts in direct taxes have been entirely paid for by the cuts in the generosity of benefits . . . the overwhelming majority of the bottom half . . . have lost; the overwhelming majority of the top 30% have gained.

This pattern of income being shifted from poor to rich is repeated again by the introduction of the poll tax. As a flat-rate tax on individuals it falls more heavily on poor than rich people. Figures from the Institute for Fiscal Studies show that households with a net household income (adjusted for family size) of under £100 a week lost £1.30 a week in the changeover from rates to the poll tax. This loss increased to £3.85 a week for a household with a net income of £200-£250 a week. This is because rebates run out at this stage. Meanwhile households with a net income of £600-£1,000 a week gained £4.04 a week, and those with an income of £1,000-plus a week gained £6.50 a week. [9]

Wealth

Wealth has to be distinguished from income. But shares of wealth are rarely discussed. Although inequalities in wealth have been reduced in recent years, its distribution remains extremely unequal (see Table 28). [10] In 1966 the wealthiest 10% owned 69% of marketable wealth, while the least wealthy 50% owned a mere 3%. By 1987 the wealthiest 10% had seen their share drop to 50% of marketable wealth and the bottom 50% rise to 7%. Between 1979 and 1987 wealth was redistributed from the very rich to the fairly rich (due mainly to the rise in home-ownership and savings) – the bottom half of society's share rose just 2 percentage points. The poorest half of society still hold virtually no wealth at all and the gulf between the poorest half of society and the top is still vast.

TABLE 28
Distribution of marketable wealth

Percentage of wealth owned by:

	1966	1976	1979	1986	1987
Most wealthy 1%	33	24	24	18	18
Most wealthy 10%	69	61	59	50	50
Least wealthy 50%	3	5	5	6	7

SOURCE: Inland Revenue Statistics, 1989, Table 10.5, HMSO, 1989 and 1982, Table 4.8, HMSO, 1982

Owning your own home has become an increasingly important source of personal wealth. In 1971 housing was one-fifth of all personal wealth, but by 1988 it was a third. Now nearly two-thirds of people own their own homes. [11] This boom in home-ownership will have a significant impact on inheritance patterns in years to come. But the expansion of owner occupation has crucial consequences for the third of society who cannot afford to buy their own homes. Peter Willmott and Alan Murie describe the polarisation of housing in Britain today: [12]

> In the last decade or so the picture has changed. Council housing as a whole has become more and more the preserve of poor people. And within the council sector the poorest and most disadvantaged have more and more had to live on the worst estates. Britain is splitting into two nations: a majority living in decent houses which they own themselves and a minority condemned to the worst of the stock.
>
> This process of splitting up is called 'polarisation'. It matters because poor people are living on housing estates that are so decrepit, vandalised and unsafe as to be below acceptable standards. It matters, too, because people living there feel helpless, looked down on by others as inferior.

The third of society who are excluded from owning a home and thereby holding this form of wealth are forced to rely on a shrinking and impoverished public and privately rented sector.

Conclusion

Rich and poor are more sharply divided than ever. Even after tax and benefits and family size are taken into account, in 1987 the poorest fifth held just 7.6% of all household income; the richest fifth held over five times as much – 43%. Changes in taxation and social security policies have brought a *declining* share of the national income to the poor and a *rising* share to the affluent. The danger is that social policies are reinforcing divisions and the exclusion experienced by the people who are living in and on the margins of poverty.

The task of tackling inequality lies in many different areas of policy. A more progressive tax system, an employment and training strategy which puts tackling unemployment at the forefront, a statutory minimum wage and more generous benefits, would begin to tackle the inequalities that beset our society.

NOTES

1. *Daily Telegraph*, 25 March 1985.
2. *Economic Trends*, HMSO, May 1990, see tables.
3. *see* note 2.
4. *General Household Survey 1987*, Tables 8C and 8D, HMSO, 1990.
5. *The new review*, Low Pay Unit, No 1, December/January 1990.
6. M Dixon, *Financial Times*, 29 August 1990.
7. *House of Commons Hansard*, 3 April 1990, cols 524-6.
8. J Hills, *Changing tax: how the tax system works and how to change it*, CPAG Ltd, 1990.
9. M Ridge and S Smith, *Local government finance, 1990 Reforms*, Institute for Fiscal Studies, 1990; and P Esam and C Oppenheim, *A Charge on the Community*, CPAG Ltd and LGIU, 1989.
10. *Inland Revenue Statistics 1989*, HMSO, 1989.
11. P Ormerod and M Wilmott, 'Willpower: homeownership, inheritance & the next century', *Poverty* 73, CPAG Ltd, 1989.
12. P Willmott and A Murie, *Polarisation and social housing*, Policy Studies Institute, 1988.

Conclusion

Poverty blights the lives of a fifth of Britain's population and around a quarter of its children. The evidence amassed in these pages shows how poverty multiplied more'rapidly between 1975 and 1985 than in any other country in the European Community. It shows how Northern Ireland, the North, the North-West, Yorkshire and Humberside, the Midlands and some inner cities have been ravaged by unemployment. It shows how unemployment and single parenthood bring high risks of poverty. It shows how poverty seeps into people's lives – endangering their homes and their health. It shows how Britain has become more unequal than at any time since the Second World War and how the poorest have had only the barest share of rising prosperity. It shows how our society excludes millions from full participation in society. It exposes the way in which the dice is loaded against millions of children, denying them the chance to fulfil their potential.

Poverty is often created when the tie to the labour market is severed – because of unemployment, or caring for another person at home, or because of disability. But access to the labour market does not in itself guarantee escape from poverty. Often employment provides only low, insecure or sporadic earnings. Poverty is also intensified when the extra costs of having a child, coping with a disability or caring for an elderly relative are not met adequately by earnings or social security benefits. Such poverty is not random but shaped by class, by gender and by race.

Policies to tackle poverty have to respond to several challenges:

- **demographic pressures** – the greater numbers of elderly, and especially very old people with greater disabilities;
- **economic changes** – higher unemployment, changing work patterns, low wages, growing inequality, and the concentration of poverty among black and other ethnic minority communities;
- **social changes** – shifting patterns of family life, especially the increase in the proportion of women with children in paid work and the rise in the number of single parents;

- a **crisis of confidence** in the capacity of welfare provided by the state to deal with poverty.

Grappling with these challenges takes place against the background of a social security system which seems to have lost its way. It also takes place in a new context in which the focus is on the European Community.

Beveridge's post-war vision of social security to meet people's needs from cradle to grave has been severely undermined both by changes in society and by specific policies. The mainstay of Beveridge's social security scheme was national insurance: those in full-time paid work (largely men and single women) were to be catered for during interruptions to their work (unemployment, sickness etc) and after retirement. Others (women and children) were to be provided for as 'dependants' of the male breadwinner. But such a model no longer fits reality. Recent policies have weakened or abolished some key benefits (such as the freeze in child benefit and the abolition of the maternity grant) and have withdrawn certain rights. Over the last ten years, the marked shift towards means-testing in conjunction with the rise in unemployment has brought staggering numbers into the maze of means-testing, with its complexity, discretion, and delays. The ability of some parts of the social security system to function adequately has been called into question.

The approach of a single market in the European Community in 1992 brings the threat of increased inequalities not only between countries in Europe, but also *within* the countries themselves. The 'social dimension' of Europe is at present but a pale counterpart of the economic dimension. The Community Charter of Fundamental Social Rights, which sets out important rights for workers, is flawed by being restricted primarily to the rights of people in employment – excluding racial discrimination – and by not being binding on member states. [1]

In the light of all these changes, what kind of strategy should we be pursuing in the United Kingdom to prevent poverty?

First, it must be a comprehensive strategy. The task of tackling poverty lies in many different areas of government responsibility, in policies for industry and the regions, for housing, education, social services and transport, for the environment and energy, as well as in the traditional areas of employment, social security and taxation. We only touch briefly on the broader areas here. We focus on three principal tools for tackling poverty and redistributing resources:

- improving access to the labour market and conditions within it;
- improving the benefits which support those who are either not in paid work or who work part time;
- making the tax system fairer.

Employment, social security and taxation policies are the central tools for sharing out resources more fairly between rich and poor, healthy and sick, white people and black people, employed and unemployed, able-bodied and disabled and between men and women.

As the pages of *Poverty: the Facts* reveal, poverty denies people the chance of achieving their potential. Thus, the framework for any anti-poverty policy must be to give people the bricks on which to build their future and the future for their children. These bricks include: a decent home, a comprehensive and free health system, free education, subsidised childcare, cheap public transport, an insulation and energy saving programme, and a healthy environment.

> The wages, social security and tax system should, together, ensure that all members of society have sufficient income to enable them to meet their public and private obligations as citizens and exercise effectively their legal, political and social rights as citizens
>
> (CPAG's Charter for Social Citizenship)[2]

More specifically, CPAG urges active steps towards the following policies.[3]

Employment

> Of course the creation of wealth is important . . . but the question remains for what is that wealth to be used? The well-being of all members of that society cannot just be an incidental consequence of an economic policy but must be an integral part of the overall policy which decides in which direction our society should be heading. Only in this way can a proper relationship be reached between economic and social policy.   (*Not Just for the Poor*)[4]

Formulating a strategy for employment lies at the heart of policies to reduce poverty. Employment policies should be about access to employment, about ensuring both flexibility and security for the workforce, about promoting anti-discrimination in employment and about preventing poverty at work. Such policies should include:

- Employment rights which apply equally to full and part time workers including a statutory minimum wage.
- Provisions to enable women and men to combine paid work with caring responsibilities at home – increased access to childcare facilities for both under school age and school-aged children which provide a stimulating environment for children; equal pay for women and men.
- Access to decent jobs and training for all, especially groups who

experience discrimination in employment – women, black people and other ethnic minorities, unskilled workers, people with disabilities and long-term unemployed people.

- Endorsement of the European draft directives which improve the rights of parents and women at work – parental leave and leave for family reasons, pro-rata rights for part-time and temporary workers, and extended maternity rights for women leaving and returning to work.

Social Security

As we see it, social security has wider aims than the prevention or relief of poverty. It is the response to an aspiration for security in its widest sense. Its fundamental purpose is to give individuals and families the confidence that their level of living and quality of life will not, in so far as is possible, be greatly eroded by any social or economic eventuality. This involves not just meeting needs as and when they arise but also preventing risks from arising in the first place, and helping individuals and families to make the best possible adjustment when faced with disabilities and disadvantages which have not been or could not be prevented.   (*Into the 21st Century*)[5]

The principles which should underpin social security are:

- Solidarity – collective security against risks, such as unemployment or sickness.
- The sharing by society as a whole of the responsibility for caring for children, elderly people and people with disabilities.
- Preventing poverty, rather than patching over it.

These principles mean a social security system which would provide:

- Adequate benefits to meet people's needs – physical, social and cultural – to enable people to participate fully in society. Benefits should be paid, as far as possible, without means tests and contribution tests.
- Individual autonomy – benefits paid on an individual basis so that women as well as men can claim benefits in their own right.
- Equal access and treatment regardless of sex, race, marital status or sexual orientation.
- Clear rights to benefits, which should be administered efficiently and humanely by sufficient staff.
- Simplicity – benefits should be easy to understand and administer.
- Flexibility – benefits should be paid in a way which includes those working part time within the social security system and in a way which takes account of cultural differences.

Above all, it is essential that the social security system caters for everyone rather than just people in poverty. This means moving away from the means-test and targeting. This is the only way to guarantee that social security does not become a second-class service for the most vulnerable.

> We are only likely to be able to meet the needs of the weak and vulnerable – which may include all of us at different points of our lives – if the services recognise their special needs and do not push them to the margins of society. In justifying this conclusion, we must return once again to the basic truths which we believe must underlie any system of welfare. It must be concerned with the well-being of all members of society: the notion of interdependence and concern for the poor and oppressed demands no less. Any model which splits off the least fortunate members of society and treats them in a way which is fundamentally different from the rest is unacceptable.
>
> *(Not only for the Poor)*[6]

Taxation

> Income, wealth and social welfare are unequally distributed in all OECD countries, and redistribution is an objective of society and the State . . . There is a well established role for the welfare state which is firmly rooted in the idea of market failure and the desire for redistributional justice.
>
> *(Social Expenditure 1960-90)*[7]

Taxation policies determine how much income people can keep out of their earnings or benefits and they are one of the principal means of redistributing income and wealth from rich to poor. Fairer policies on taxation should include:

- Creating a more progressive tax structure.
- Fully independent taxation for men and women, which does not depend on marital status.
- A local tax system which reflects ability to pay with the reintroduction of 100% rebates for those on the lowest incomes.

As well as these broad policies CPAG believes that it essential for governments to commit themselves to:

- research into people's basic physical and social needs in order to provide the foundation for a poverty line and a rationale for adequate benefits
- the publication of annual statistics on low incomes

Only then will all governments be compelled to publicly recognise the existence of poverty and develop policies to combat it.

As inequalities have grown and poverty has become more pressing and more intense, there has been strong public support for policies which tackle these injustices. The 1990/1 *British Social Attitudes Survey* revealed that:

- three-quarters of people believe that income differences in Britain are too large;
- only a quarter (26%) thought that large income differences were necessary for national prosperity;
- nearly two thirds support action to reduce income differences (63%);
- 82% thought that government should spend more on benefits for the poor.[8]

An earlier *Social Attitudes Survey* shows that the proportion of people prepared to pay increased taxes to finance welfare services has grown from a third to nearly half between 1983 and 1986.[9] Such surveys reveal that the welfare state retains enduring popularity despite cuts and changes. It has beome fashionable to argue that the problem of poverty, low pay and unemployment can only be tackled after the development of a strong and stable economy. That to put concerns about poverty before economic development is to put the cart before the horse. However, CPAG is convinced that long-term economic growth must go hand in hand with social justice. That only a society which is not wrought by social division and the exclusion of the poor can provide the foundations for stability and growth. There is also a strong conviction that our society is scarred by injustice; a conviction which goes hand in hand with an equally firm belief that something should be done about it. It is on such attitudes that we have to build.

The living standards of the majority in the United Kingdom continue to flourish, yet a substantial minority of the population is living in poverty. It is this divide which must be addressed with urgency by the general public, by political parties and above all by governments.

As part of CPAG 's twenty-fifth anniversary we call for *freedom from poverty and social rights for all*. This rallying call echoes the sentiments of many others:

> It is only so far as poverty is abolished that freedom is increased.
>
> Harold Macmillan, *The Middle Way*[10]

> Social rights liberate people from insecurity, and that is why the new debate about citizenship must begin with such unambiguous social rights at the right

not to fall below a certain level of income and the right to an education . . .
The pressure for extending citizenship rights in our own societies is going to
be very strong. It will be increased by the fact that the fledgling democracies
in East Europe have rediscovered the same principle. I would not be surprised
at all if this became a decade of citizenship rights.

Sir Ralf Dahrendorf, *Decade of the Citizen*[11]

NOTES

1. *Charter for fundamental social rights*, European Commission, 1989.
2. R Lister, *The exclusive society: citizenship and the poor*, CPAG Ltd, 1990.
3. These policies come from a variety of sources, in particular from R Lister, *There is an alternative*, CPAG Ltd, 1987; and the *Social Charter* in R Lister, *Exclusive society: citizenship and the poor*, CPAG Ltd, 1990.
4. *Not just for the poor: christian perspectives on the welfare state*, Church House Publishing, 1986.
5. *Into the 21st Century*, International Labour Office, 1984.
6. *see* note 4.
7. *Social expenditure 1960-1990*, OECD, 1985.
8. Ed R Jowell et al, *British social attitudes*, special international report, 6th Report, Social and Community Planning Research, Gower, 1990.
9. Ed R Jowell et al, *British social attitudes*, the 1987 Report, Social and Community Planning, Gower, 1987.
10. H Macmillan, *The Middle Way*, 1962.
11. Sir Ralf Dahrendorf, *Decade of the citizen*, Guardian, 1 August 1990.

Definitions and terms

Average: is a single number that is intended to be representative of a set of numbers. There are different kinds of average – mean, median and mode. In *Poverty: the facts* only the mean and median are used. The **mean** is when all the numbers are added up and then the total is divided by the number of numbers. The **median** is the mid-point of any range of numbers. The mean is less stable than the median as it tends to be dragged up by higher incomes. In the government figures – *Households below Average Income* – people's incomes are measured as a proportion of the mean income. In Chapter 8, the *European Community Survey* uses the mean, whereas the Luxembourg Income Study uses the median.

Benefit Assessment Unit: individual or couple, with or without children, on which entitlement to supplementary benefit or income support is based (*see* Low Income Families).

Child: In the government figures – *Households below Average Income* and *Low Income Families* – a child is defined as anyone aged under 16, or 16-19 if s/he is in full-time non-advanced education.

Community charge benefit: also known as poll tax rebate. This replaced the rate rebate which was payable under housing benefit. It covers a maximum of 80% of the community charge/poll tax.

Decile groups: successive tenths of all households arranged by income from bottom to top.

Equivalence scales: are used to adjust income to take account of different family or household sizes. This is done in order to reflect the extent to which families or households require different incomes to achieve the same standard of living. The scales give different weights to adults and children. For example: a two-parent family with two children has an income of £200 a week. Assuming that a couple has a weight of 1.00 and each child 0.5, when income is **equivalised**, it is £100 a week (£200 divided by 2.00). There is a great deal of controversy about which equivalence scales are appropriate – eg, how much weight to place on children's needs at different ages. The government's *Households below*

Average Income statistics use different equivalence scales from those used in *Low Income Families*.

Family credit: is a means-tested social security benefit for families with children in low-paid work (for 24 hours a week or more). It replaced family income supplement as part of the 1986 Social Security Act (fully implemented in 1988).

Family expenditure survey: is conducted annually by the Central Statistical Office. The *Family Expenditure Survey* is a survey of people's expenditure and income in the United Kingdom.

Households below average income (HBAI): was produced by the Department of Social Security for the first time in 1988 and has replaced the *Low Income Families* statistics. HBAI is based on an analysis of the *Family Expenditure Survey*. HBAI measures the numbers of people living on incomes below the average (the mean). The HBAI figures are for Britain and not the United Kingdom, thus excluding Northern Ireland. HBAI uses **household** income which is adjusted for household size (equivalised) and then divided by the numbers of individuals in the household. Income is **current** (ie, the income stated at the time of the **Family Expenditure Survey** interview). Income is defined as: net earnings after income tax, national insurance and superannuation, gross profit from self-employment, all social security benefits including housing benefit, maintenance, investment income, and some income in kind, such as luncheon vouchers, less income tax and national insurance paid direct. The statistics show income before and after housing costs. Housing costs are defined as: rent and rates, water rates, ground rent and service charges, mortgage interest and structural insurance for home owners. CPAG argues that one possible poverty line is 50% of average income.

Housing benefit: is a means-tested social security benefit which helps people on low incomes in and out of work with their housing costs.

Housing benefit supplement: under the social security system prior to 1988, housing benefit supplement was paid to claimants whose income was below supplementary benefit level after paying their housing costs. It was complex and had a very low rate of take-up.

Income: can be measured in a number of different ways. See *Households below Average Income* and *Low Income Families* for definitions used in these series. In Chapter 9, figures are used from the government's Central Statistical Office publication *Economic Trends*. We have picked out two measures of income: original income (ie, income before taxes and benefits) and post-tax income (ie, income after direct (eg, income tax and national insurance) and indirect taxes (ie, VAT) and cash benefits).

Income support: is a social security benefit which is supposed to provide a minimum income for people who are not in full-time work who meet certain conditions. It is means-tested. It replaced supplementary benefit as part of the 1986 Social Security Act (implemented in 1988) – see Social Security Act 1986.

Institute for fiscal studies: is an educational charity which promotes research and discussion of tax and finance matters. It has undertaken a great deal of work on behalf of the Social Services (now Social Security) Select Committee in looking at the distribution of low income. It has produced its own estimates of the Low Income Families statistics because of the government's decision to stop publishing them.

Low income families (LIF): was produced by the Department of Health and Social Security for the last time in 1988. These were based on the Family Expenditure Survey. LIF showed the numbers of people living on a low income – below 140% of supplementary benefit. The figures are just for Britain and not Northern Ireland. The Social Services (now Social Security) Select Committee has commissioned the Institute for Fiscal Studies to continue publishing this series. CPAG argues that one possible poverty line is the supplementary benefit level. LIF makes different assumptions about income from HBAI. It uses: **family** income based on the Benefit Assessment Unit (see above) (rather than **household** income, as used in HBAI); **normal** income (rather than **current** income, as is used in HBAI). Normal income means that if the head of the household is off from work because of unemployment or sickness for less than 3 months at the time of the Family Expenditure Survey interview, the income in employment is used rather than the current income. In LIF there is an allowance for travel to work costs for full-time workers. Income is defined as: net earnings after tax, national insurance, and superannuation, gross profit from self-employment, all social security benefits excluding housing benefit, maintenance, investment income, and some income in kind, such as luncheon vouchers, less tax and national insurance paid direct. The statistics show income after housing costs. Housing costs are defined as: rent and rates (net of rebates), water rates, ground rent and service charges, mortgage interest, supplementary benefit repairs and insurance allowance for owner-occupiers, less contributions to housing from other members of the household. LIF also uses different equivalence scales from HBAI (*see* Equivalence Scales).

Low pay: defined by the Low Pay Unit as two-thirds of male median earnings. (*see* Average). In 1989 this was £157 a week, or £4.16 an hour.

Low pay unit: is an independent body which carries out research in the field of low pay and working conditions and offers advice on rights at work.

Median: *see* Average.

Poverty definitions: CPAG uses two possible definitions of poverty: the numbers living on and below supplementary benefit and the numbers living below 50% of average income.

Quintile group: successive fifths of all households arranged by income from bottom to top.

Single parents: throughout the text we use single parents to refer to anyone who is bringing up children on their own whether they are divorced, separated, widowed or never married.

Single payments: were grants for one-off needs such as cookers, beds and furniture, which provided extra help for people living on supplementary benefit. They were replaced by the discretionary social fund in April 1988 as part of the 1986 Social Security Act (*see* Social Fund).

Social affairs unit: a research and educational trust which analyses social affairs in order to promote 'a free and orderly society in which enterprise can flourish'.

Social fund: replaced the single payments scheme in the Social Security Act 1986 (*see* Single Payments). The first part of the social fund was implemented in 1987 and provides grants for cold weather, maternity and funeral needs. It is governed by regulations and there is a legal right of appeal. The second part of the social fund was implemented in 1988; this mainly provides interest free loans and has a small budget for community care grants to prevent people going into institutional care or to help them when they leave such care. Loans are repayable directly from income support at rates of 15% in most cases (though it can be lower). This part of the social fund is discretionary and cash-limited and there is no right to an independent appeal, only to a review.

Social Security Act 1986:   was the outcome of the 'Fowler Reviews' set up to examine the options for the major reform of the social security system. The Act brought in a new structure of social security that was fully implemented in April 1988. Income support replaced supplementary benefit, the social fund replaced single payments, family credit replaced family income support and housing benefit was reduced.

Social Services Select Committee (now Social Security Select Committee): is a House of Commons Select Committee composed of MPs from all political parties. Its responsibility is to monitor issues related to social services (and now social security).

Supplementary benefit: was paid to people who were not in full-time work and who met certain conditions. It was replaced by income support as part of the Social Security Act 1986 in 1988. Supplementary benefit is used by CPAG as one possible poverty line.

Unemployment unit: is an independent body which campaigns on, and does research into, unemployment and training.

Wages councils: known as Trade Boards, were first set up in 1909. Trade Boards determine minimum rates of pay and conditions, backed up by the force of law, in certain low-paying industries such as retailing, hairdressing, laundries and clothing. The councils are made up of members from the employers, and trade unions, and independent members. Their powers were weakened in 1986 and until recently they were under the threat of abolition. The government now says that are still 'under review'.

SOURCES: DSS, Households below Average Income: a statistical analysis, 1981-1987, Government Statistical Services, 1990, see notes and technical annex; DHSS, Low Income Families 1985, Government Statistical Service, 1988; J Hills, Changing tax: the tax system and how to change it, CPAG Ltd, 1989.

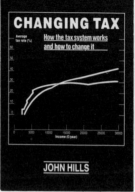

Now's the time to join CPAG!

1965-1990

CHILD POVERTY ACTION GROUP **25 YEARS** *Working against poverty*

We can help you ... with the facts on poverty.
You can help us ... in the fight against poverty.

CPAG membership gives you access to all the latest – on welfare rights, income inequalities, perspectives on policy, and lots more!

And CPAG members give us the support we need to ensure that poverty is at the heart of the agenda, whatever political party is in power.

Send off the form now, and join CPAG in our 25th anniversary year.

Please complete and send to: CPAG, 4th Floor, 1–5 Bath Street, London EC1V 9PY.

- -

I would like to join CPAG as a comprehensive member . . . . ❏
(Comprehensive members receive CPAG's regular journal, *Poverty*, plus welfare rights and social policy publications – for £35/year or £40 from January 1991).

or I would like information about other membership options . . . ❏

I enclose a donation to CPAG of £ . . . . ❏

I enclose a cheque/p.o. (made out to CPAG) for £35 . . . . ❏

Name _____

Organisation (if applicable) _____

Address _____

_____

_____ Postcode _____